But you are not to be called rabbi, for you have but one teacher, and you are all students. And call no one your father, for you have one Father — the one in heaven. Nor are you to be called instructors, for you have but one instructor, the Messiah. The greatest among you will be your servant. All who exalt themselves will be humbled, and all who humble themselves will be exalted.

MATTHEW 23:8-11

"ONE TEACHER"

Doctrinal Authority in the Church

Le Groupe des Dombes

Translated by
Catherine E. Clifford

WILLIAM B. EERDMANS PUBLISHING COMPANY

GRAND RAPIDS, MICHIGAN / CAMBRIDGE, U.K.

First published in 2005 as *"Un seul Maître"*: *L'autorité doctrinale dans l'Église* by Bayard.

This English edition © 2010 by William B. Eerdmans Publishing Company

Published 2010 by
Wm. B. Eerdmans Publishing Co.
2140 Oak Industrial Drive N.E., Grand Rapids, Michigan 49505 /
P.O. Box 163, Cambridge CB3 9PU U.K.

Printed in the United States of America

16 15 14 13 12 11 10   7 6 5 4 3 2 1

Library of Congress Cataloging-in-Publication Data

"Un seul maître": *L'autorité doctrinale dans l'Église.*
"One teacher": doctrinal authority in the church /
Le Groupe des Dombes; translated by Catherine E. Clifford.
p.   cm.
Includes bibliographical references.
ISBN 978-0-8028-2598-8 (pbk.: alk. paper)
1. Authority — Religious aspects — Christianity. 2. Authority —
Religious aspects — Catholic Church.
I. Clifford, Catherine E., 1958- II. Groupe des Dombes. III. Title.

BT88.S48 2010
262'.8 — dc22
2009043678

www.eerdmans.com

In memory of
Pasteur Alain Blancy
and Père Bruno Chenu,
co-presidents of the Groupe des Dombes,
who now rest in the peace of God.

Contents

Contents

Contents

Foreword

The Groupe des Dombes has been silent since the publication of its document on Mary in 1999. Since then, it has experienced two painful losses. One after the other, after similar illnesses, its two co-presidents were prematurely called to God: Pastor Alain Blancy in September 2000, and Père Bruno Chenu in May 2003. As a sign of gratitude for their ecumenical commitment, for the faithful service rendered to the Groupe des Dombes over many years of participation, and for their leadership by virtue of their office, we dedicate these pages to them. Though we do not mention them in the list of signatories, we can say that each of them has contributed greatly to this undertaking and we have no doubt that they would have signed it, had they remained among us.

Through the years our group has been transformed and renewed. The departure of the Cistercian monks from the Abbey of Notre Dame des Dombes led us to make our home at the Benedictine Abbey of Les Pradines, where we are warmly welcomed and supported by the prayer of a fervent community. An unwritten rule — almost all the "rules" of our little group are unwritten — that one depart at the age of 75, or at the conclusion of a project, has been faithfully respected, allowing the cooptation of new members who are fully active. The group has welcomed the participation of five women and this number will surely increase in future. We remain undoubtedly a group of Western Christians, Catholics and Protestants, with no Orthodox members. Yet we remain open to the Eastern perspective on things and are ready to invite Orthodox experts, as we have in the past, to ensure that their voice is heard. In this same period, we have witnessed an important increase in attention to interreligious dialogue. Our conviction is that this in no way means the urgency of ecumenical dialogue has become outmoded. Though mindful of the connection between ecumenical and interreligious dialogue, we respect the obvious specificity of each.

Why have we chosen to examine a subject as difficult and sensitive as that of doctrinal authority in the church? Because to us it seems to be a central and sensitive point in the dialogue between the churches. The patient journey toward visible unity cannot move forward as long as this question has not been carefully thought through, for it underlies a number of other issues and will determine their possible resolution. We do not hide the fact that when it comes to this subject, to repeat an expression that is found in these pages, we have "our backs to the wall." Two other factors came together to move us in this direction: first, the tensions experienced recently in reaction to the manner and tone of certain doctrinal positions asserted on the Catholic side, with, as a counterpoint, a tendency to relativize all forms of doctrinal authority on the part of Reformation churches; and second, the great hope represented by the official signing of the Lutheran–Roman Catholic Joint Declaration on the Doctrine of Justification by Faith. The reader should not be surprised to find repeated references to this text in these chapters. This new step is in keeping with the broad ecclesiological direction of our previous documents: eucharist, ministry, sacraments, ministry of communion in the universal church, and the conversion of the churches.

The method of our work has remained the same, though we have also made room for new approaches. Beginning with several presentations, we progressively put together a schema which was fleshed out from year to year and evolved in stages through seven successive drafts. We have kept to the pattern of treating history before turning to the Scriptures. In fact, the research in these two areas was carried out simultaneously, with each enriching the other. It is worth recalling here that our approach accords an important place to prayer as part of our common life during our meetings and in an extended companionship throughout the years. These factors, which the reader will perhaps not easily discern in the writing of our texts, are essential to our work and enable it to be productive. The Groupe des Dombes is a place of transparent ecumenical encounter where members speak freely with one another. On could imagine that the theme of doctrinal authority might become the occasion for confrontations or mutual criticism, with members pointing to the weakness in the workings of the partner churches, to the point of describing a real caricature. There was nothing of the sort. On the contrary, each member sought to enter into the other's point of view in order to better understand and learn from it. Each of us has become more conscious of the need for a conversion of all the churches in this matter.

We cannot hide the relatively technical character of this document, as is evidenced already by its length. This was inevitable given the complexity of the topic. It is not possible to approach such a difficult subject with a few generous banalities that would be consigned to meaninglessness. The complexity of the problem derives particularly from the fact that Catholics and Protestants agree on the fundamental points of reference for doctrinal authority (texts, persons, communities, etc.), yet we regard the relationship among these points of reference very differently. The ground of our consensus is the very basis of divergence. This insight directed the elaboration of chapters IV and V. We also refer constantly to the three ecclesiological dimensions — personal, collegial, and communal — identified in the 1927 report of Faith and Order in Lausanne and often repeated in our documents. We see them illustrated perfectly in our common history, prior to the rupture of the sixteenth century, and totally founded in the Scriptures.

The public to whom we address ourselves is very diverse. We always intend to speak to all the baptized in our churches, for the working of doctrinal authority concerns them, first and foremost. Yet we also desire that our reflection be theologically credible, and thus, historically well founded. Finally, we hope that the authorities of our churches will attend to our work, examining themselves as to its pertinence, and drawing inspiration in their pastoral practice and in the context of the official ecumenical dialogues that they promote. For this reason we have used different fonts in the two historical chapters. The reader can easily follow the line of argumentation and understand the conclusions by reading only the normal print in the body of the text. Those who wish to verify the precise historical information on which our argument is based will be interested to read the finer print in the indented sections.

It is our wish that this document, written in good faith, be received in our churches for what it is, in the hope that we have been faithful to the Pauline conviction: "I do it all for the sake of the gospel" (1 Cor. 9:23).

PÈRE BERNARD SESBOÜÉ   PASTEUR JEAN TARTIER

Abbreviations

ARCIC	Anglican-Roman Catholic International Commission
BA	*Bibliothèque augustinienne.* Paris: DDB.
CH	Irénée de Lyon, *Contre les hérésies.* Trad. A. Rousseau. Paris: Cerf, 1984.
CO	*Calvini opera quae supersunt omnia.* Edited by Baum, Chemnitz, Reuss. Corpus Reformatorum. Brunschwick: Schwetske, 1863-1900.
DHGE	*Dictionnaire d'histoire et de géographie ecclésiastiques.* Paris: Letouzey et Ané, 1967.
DV	Second Vatican Council, Dogmatic Constitution on Divine Revelation, *Dei Verbum*
HE	*Histoire ecclésiastique* (Eusèbe)
LG	Second Vatican Council, Dogmatic Constitution on the Church, *Lumen Gentium*
PG	*Patrologia graeca* (J.-P. Migne), Paris.
PL	*Patrologia Latina* (J.-P. Migne), Paris.
SC	*Sources chrétiennes.* Lyon et Paris: Le Cerf.
UR	Second Vatican Council, Decree on Ecumenism, *Unitatis Redintegratio*
WA	*Weimarer Ausgabe.* Köln: Bölhaus, 1981. The German edition of the complete works of Martin Luther.

Introduction

Why Authority?

1. In our society authority presents a problem. This is a consequence of the profound cultural change that we are experiencing, whereby a number of the foundations upon which the traditional exercise of authority once rested are disappearing — a change accompanied by the rise of individualism as an ultimate value. An effort to take into account the reality of cultural pluralism further accentuates this difficulty. In the wake of the violent protest against authority in the West in the 1960s and subsequent years, many espouse a position of indifference or of relativizing civil, political, spiritual, or moral authorities. Politics is often discredited and participation in unions, associations, religious groups is less common than in former times. In short, our world is witnessing a crisis of authority.

2. Perhaps inevitably, authority is also problematic in our churches. In the past, they not only exercised a commonly accepted authority over the faithful, they exercised a certain moral authority over society. This is no longer the case. While Catholics, or perhaps a majority of them, maintain an attitude of obedience and trust in relation to ecclesial authority, they are immersed in a liberal culture marked by a critical hermeneutic. There is an even greater correlation between the relativization of authority and Protestant culture. The Protestant community is so diverse that a deficit of authority constitutes a handicap for the witness of these Christian communities. Thus, one can also say that there is a crisis of authority in our churches.

3. These present difficulties impel us to look back at history and to the sources of ecclesial life. The New Testament bears witness to the ways in which the apostolic church overcame diverse crises. Moreover, the problem of authority arose regularly in the history of the church, each time there was a crisis in society. We encounter this phenomenon notably in the grave example of the sixteenth century. Certain abuses of authority and power in the medieval church were among the causes of the irrepressible development of the Reformation and the breakdown of ecclesial unity. The exercise of authority, therefore, constitutes an eminently ecumenical theme for reflection.

4. Nonetheless, authority is not to be considered only as a problem in the functioning of the church. It is first and foremost understood as a gift given by Christ to his church: "All authority in heaven and on earth has been given me. Go, therefore, and make disciples of all the nations, baptizing them in the name of the Father and the Son and the Holy Spirit, and teaching them to obey everything that I have commanded you" (Matt. 28:19). This is why authority is of interest to people of faith. This gift is ordered to salvation; that is to say, it is intended to serve the greatest good that God desires for men and women of our world.

5. It is not our intention to consider all the problems posed by authority in the life of the churches, for such an undertaking would be enormous. The present work is limited to the study of *doctrinal authority,* that is, the church's mission to proclaim and teach what it has received from Christ.

6. Indeed, we have touched upon the general theme of authority in our previous treatment of the question of ministries,[1] and we will not revisit that aspect now. Yet we consider the question of the exercise of doctrinal authority to be an acute problem today. It involves the credibility of preaching and of the transmission of the faith. Even the Corin-

---

1. *Pour une réconciliation des ministères* (Presses de Taizé, 1973); *Le ministère épiscopal* (Presses de Taizé, 1976); *Le ministère de communion dans l'Église universelle* (Paris: Centurion, 1986). All three documents are found in *Pour la communion des Églises. L'apport du Groupe des Dombes, 1937-1987* (Paris: Centurion, 1988). [English translations: "Towards a Reconciliation of Ministries," in *Modern Ecumenical Agreements on the Ministry,* ed. H. R. McAdoo, trans. Pamela Gaughan (London: SPCK, 1975), pp. 87-107; "The Episcopal Ministry. Reflections and Proposals Concerning the Ministry of Vigilance and Unity in the Particular Church," *One in Christ* 14 (1978): 267-88.]

thians criticized Paul, saying they found "his speech contemptible" (2 Cor. 10:10). The churches of today are confronted by an analogous situation and experience serious contradictions.

7. Part of the difficulty concerns language. Ecclesial discourse seems to be exiled to the margins of our culture. It is increasingly difficult for the churches to make themselves understood. Yet this problem is also related to the way in which ecclesial institutions function, which in itself is a kind of language. On the other hand, not all the means and levels of expression are vested with the same authority. Lastly, we are confronted with the problem of the "hierarchy of truths."[2]

8. In the area of authority, the Catholic Church and the churches of the Reformation have followed very different, if not divergent paths. For this reason, it is necessary to get to the heart of the problem by examining the basis for the gift of authority, by analyzing its role in the mystery of the church and in the concrete structures of the churches, and also by studying the ways they function. A perfectly legitimate and well-founded authority can "become derailed" in the way it is exercised and so contradict the gospel witness on which it is founded.

9. In short, how far do we diverge in our conception of authority? We want to have the courage to go right to the root of the problem and to really challenge each other. We also hope to identify a number of signposts that might guide us on the path toward ecclesial reconciliation.

Authority and Power

10. Before presenting an outline of this document, it is useful to identify several elements that distinguish between the understanding of authority and power in society and in the church.

2. Theologians must "remember that in Catholic doctrine there exists an order or 'hierarchy' of truths, since they vary in their connection with the foundation of the Christian faith." Second Vatican Council, "Decree on Ecumenism," in *Decrees of the Ecumenical Councils,* vol. II, ed. Norman P. Tanner (Georgetown: Georgetown University Press, 1990), no. 11, p. 915. See also Groupe des Dombes, *Marie dans le dessein de Dieu et la communion des saints* (Paris: Bayard, 1999), no. 242, p. 127, n. 1. [English translation: *Mary in the Plan of God and in the Communion of Saints,* trans. Matthew J. O'Connell (New York: Paulist, 2002), p. 98.]

11. First, concerning **authority:** the word and the thing can be understood in different ways. Indeed, authority (from the Latin *auctor,* founder and instigator) excludes all recourse to physical constraint since it is exercised over subjects who recognize both the established "authorities" and the "authority" that is being exercised. Thus, one usually distinguishes two types of authority: functional authority, which is delegated and relative, and personal authority, which is charismatic and comprehensive. To be an authority who has authority: this is the ideal. For "being without having" leads to a power which is characterized by force, whereas "having without being" translates into a weakness that renders one impotent.

12. **Power** may be defined as an aptitude to undertake effective action. In itself, it is legitimate and good. Yet it is always threatened by the *abuse of power.* Whereas authority fosters conviction in others, the abuse of power seeks victory over others. In the latter case, the power of domination displaces authority as service. For this reason democracy attempts to construct and to protect the social bond and the pact of common life by entrusting power and legal means to those who have been elected to hold public authority.[3] Yet the growing complexity of factors to be taken into account in order to carry out these choices means that the "authority of competence" has a new importance, and must sometimes work together with established authority. For this reason, analysts of the contemporary context speak of a possible "degeneration of democracy" and of the passage to a state of "oligarchy" where trust is put in the specialists, thus creating the risk of a technocratic neo-clerical power held by those to whom we give credit.

---

3. Every system of power includes an irreducible tension between two poles. As Paul Ricoeur observes, a reduction to a single pole would put an end to the system: "I have always found myself caught between nonviolent utopia and the feeling that something irreducible subsists in the relationship of commanding, of governing . . . , the difficulty of joining together an asymmetrical relation and a relation of reciprocity. When . . . one is the bearer of the vertical relation, one continually seeks to give this a legitimacy drawn from horizontal relations; this legitimation, in the end, is fully authentic only if it allows the asymmetry tied to the vertical institutional relation to disappear; yet this vertical relation cannot completely disappear because it is irreducible — the agency of decision can never perfectly correspond to the ideal representation of a direct democracy, where each and every person would actually participate in every decision." *Critique and Conviction,* trans. Kathleen Blamey (New York: Columbia University Press, 1998), p. 39. Original version: *La critique et la conviction* (Paris: Calmann-Lévy, 1995), p. 65.

13. Reflecting upon these two realities, *authority* and *power,* inevitably leads us to consider their application within the institution of the church itself. It is not, it seems, the first article of the Creed that causes difficulty: "I believe in God." Neither is it the articles that develop the great Christian beliefs of the incarnation, redemption, and the action of the Holy Spirit. It is rather the confession of the "one, holy, catholic, and apostolic church." While an object of faith, the notion of the church has become most often the object of debate, and even of conflict between different conceptions of doctrinal authority, of ecclesial power, and of their exercise. Because of this, it is difficult to distinguish between that which is in conformity with our common faith and that which seems to require reform. Such a discernment must be carried out, and the need to do so is urgent.

14. Three modes of exercising of authority constantly interact in the life of the church and of Christians:

- God's supreme authority exercised in the individual conscience, in its intimate and ultimate decisions.
- The authority which proceeds from Scripture received as revelation and interpreted by the tradition.
- Lastly, the authority exercised by institutions that desire to serve and regulate Christian faith and life, the ecclesial magisterium (Catholicism) and synodal authority (Protestantism).

15. Now it is the relationship of these three modes for exercising authority — indeed, the use of power — which gives expression to what is at stake in the actual exercise of doctrinal authority. Taking into account the risks and difficulties which we have noted above helps us to situate our work within the context of the conviction that ultimately doctrinal authority in the church can only be that of the whole church in its faith and life.

16. In the past, when reflecting on the authority of Jesus — a question that is always relevant in the church which is at its service — one noted that his authority came from both a freedom of speaking and an active dynamism for announcing the reign of God and for manifesting the salvation of humanity (preaching and miracles, discourse and healings). In this perspective, the problem of doctrinal authority in the church is not only one of precise and authoritative definitions, but also

of the witness given by those in authority through the harmonization of words and deeds.

*   *   *

Following a method found to be tried and true, this study comprises five chapters:

17. *Chapters one* and *two* offer an historical overview and attempt to gather together the lessons of history concerning diverse forms of the exercise of authority and their justification. They explore the age of the Fathers of the Church, which is particularly instructive, as well as the Middle Ages. This helps us to understand the meaning of the Reformation crisis with regard to authority, and its consequences for the life of those churches born of the Reformation. Chapter two concludes with an analysis of the development of the *living magisterium* in the Catholic Church in recent centuries.[4]

18. *Chapter three* studies the witness of Scripture as the *judge* of tradition. To what extent does Scripture "authorize" the doctrinal authority of the church? An examination of the great literary corpus of the New Testament draws together its message concerning our subject.

19. *Chapter four* offers a broad range of references to doctrinal authority which the churches hold in common. Also noted is the evident diversity of the manner in which the churches relate to these various points of reference. The common ground generates both agreement and differences. Lastly, this chapter attempts to articulate a number of doctrinal and ecumenical proposals concerning the most sensitive of these points in the hope of achieving a "differentiated consensus."[5]

---

4. This inquiry has proven to be much longer, yet also richer, than we had anticipated. The file that we present includes complex historical facts that had to be analyzed with sufficient precision. For this reason, two types of characters will be used: paragraphs in regular font allow the reader to follow the essential lessons to be drawn; paragraphs that are indented and in smaller font size provide the necessary historical justification.

5. This expression has often been used to describe the content of the *Joint Declaration on the Doctrine of Justification* (Grand Rapids: Wm. B. Eerdmans, 2000), signed in 1999 by the authorities of the Catholic Church and the Lutheran World Federation. It expresses the fact that a fundamental consensus on the central matter of salvation in Christ can bear a certain number of differences in expression without harm to communion in faith, and can convert church-dividing differences into complementary ones. See especially nos. 14 and 43 of this document.

20. In *chapter five* we draw upon the solidarity that unites words and deeds, and invite our respective churches to proceed with concrete measures of conversion that will help them as they strive toward the unity which Christ desires. Shared concern for conversion to the gospel and the desire for recognition as church by our ecumenical partners should afford a new perspective on our disagreements.

The Lessons of History:
The Early and Medieval Church

21. Our aim is not to develop a complete history of the exercise of doctrinal authority in the church, but rather to identify a number of significant examples of how this authority was successively exercised. We wish to draw attention to certain decisive events in different periods of the two-thousand-year history of Christianity. We will then reflect on the significance of each of these moments for our study.

22. This historical survey will be developed in two chapters. Chapter one examines the patristic and medieval periods, remembering our common heritage. Chapter two touches first upon the lines of "protest" adopted by the churches of the Reformation, and then considers the centralizing development experienced by the Catholic Church in more modern times.

Section I: The Age of the Church Fathers

23. A major shift occurred during the patristic age with the so-called conversion of Constantine (318) and the rise of the ecumenical councils. During the first three centuries, doctrinal authority was exercised particularly in determining the canon of Scripture and in elaborating the rule of faith.[1] It was expressed primarily through the teaching re-

---

1. The "rule of truth" or "rule of faith" is an expression used by Irenaeus to sum up the normative content of the Christian faith, in particular the witness of Scripture and the Symbol of Faith or the Creed.

ceived from the great witnesses of faith speaking in the churches, churches over which bishops would soon preside. Of particular importance were the confessions of faith, the canon of Scripture, and the witness of Clement of Rome and of the three great figures: Irenaeus, Tertullian, and Origen. Note that only the first of these three is an "episkopos."

24. After the rallying of the Roman Empire to Christianity, the principal locus for the exercise of doctrinal authority became the first seven ecumenical councils which still provide the basis for doctrinal agreement between the churches of the East and West.[2] The first four of these — Nicaea (325), Constantinople I (381), Ephesus (431), and Chalcedon (451) — are recognized as having a particular authority, even to the point of being compared to the four gospels. As we shall see, the functioning of these early councils and their reception in the life of the church have several important lessons to teach us.

I. The First Three Centuries

1. The Witness of Clement of Rome Concerning the Demands of Life in the Church

25. Toward the end of the first century, there was serious dissension in the church of Corinth. The discord was so great that Clement, the bishop of Rome, thought he should intervene. He did so, not in the name of any jurisdictional authority, but as one writing to his brothers to show them the way of peace, which is also the way of faith. In his letter to the Christians at Corinth, he underlines the way in which the practice of gospel virtues — such as humility and concord, or again repentance and obedience — is a sign that they are worthy of the goodness that God, who chose and elected them, has shown. Clement also explains that each Christian is necessarily useful to the others. Using the image of an army, he explains that certain members of the church

---

2. We are not forgetting that in the cultural and theological context of their times, the councils of Ephesus and Chalcedon could not be received by all the churches (we will refer several times in the discussion which follows to the Assyrian Church of the East and the Oriental Orthodox Churches).

are called to command and teach, while others follow the instructions they are given. It is not proper to reject those who are appointed as leaders, nor is it appropriate for leaders to pretend that they are over and above the flock of Christ that they serve.

26. Considering the church's faithful to be a chosen people, Clement of Rome readily applies qualifiers that Scripture[3] reserves for the people of Israel — "God's own" and "a holy nation." These expressions point us toward the eschatological dimension of the church. Yet this same church still awaits the establishment of the reign of God that is to come, according to Christ's promise which was handed down from the apostles. The apostles are no longer present to teach this Good News. However, before they died they not only appointed men tested by the Spirit to be ministers, episkopoi and deacons; they also established the rule that others would succeed them in office. Clement adds that this was done with the approval of the whole church.[4] Certain ecclesial functions, especially that of teaching, which was the responsibility of the episkopoi and which was linked with diakonia, are in a way a constitutive of the church.

27. In writing to the church at Corinth to teach about both the ethical principles of life in Christian community and the nature of the church, does Bishop Clement do so in his own name or in the name of the community which has designated him to exercise the role of oversight? Almost a century later, in the last quarter of the second century, Bishop Denis of Corinth would write to Soter, bishop of Rome, that in the Corinthian church they continue to read the letter which Clement had written and sent long ago from Rome.[5] Does this mean that Clement was the sole author of the letter, or that he was only the redactor in the name of the church of the Romans? It is difficult to resolve this

3. At the end of the first century the New Testament had not yet been assembled, all of its books had not yet been written. Clement's reflection is based on the Hebrew Scriptures, our Old Testament.

4. See Clement of Rome, *Épître aux Corinthiens,* 42 et 44; *SC* 167 et 173. [English translation: "The Epistle to the Corinthians," in *The Epistles of St. Clement of Rome and St. Ignatius of Antioch,* Ancient Christian Writers, vol. 1, ed. J. Quaesten and J. Plumpe (Westminster, MD: Newman, 1946), pp. 34-36.]

5. Eusebius of Cesaraea, *HE,* IV, 23, 11; *SC* 31, p. 205. [English translation: *The Ecclesiastical History,* vol. 1, trans. Kirsopp Lake (Cambridge: Harvard University Press, 1926; reprinted 1992), IV, 23, 11, pp. 382-383. Subsequent citations are taken from the English version.]

question, yet the latter solution would serve to demonstrate clearly the extent to which a church which had been taught, was now teaching.

2. The Authority of the Church in the Confession of Faith and over the Canon of Scripture

28. The early Christian community takes up the name church, *ekklesia,* previously used by the Septuagint — the first Greek translation of the Old Testament[6] — to designate Israel as the people gathered together to offer the cultic worship that is due to God. Thus, it also expresses an awareness of being not only the assembly of those who believe and worship God in spirit and in truth, but also of having been chosen and elected while waiting for the second coming of Christ. Initially, the church appears "enthusiastic" in the fullest sense of the word, and Christianity emerges less as a strictly defined theology with immutable articles of faith or necessary obligations, than as the proclamation of "Good News." This Good News or gospel is the proclamation that Jesus is the Christ of God, that he has died and is risen. This is the message of the church, the center of its faith — "the faith by which we believe" *(fides qua creditur).* During their encounter on the road to Gaza, the eunuch replies to Philip: "I believe that Jesus Christ is the Son of God." Thus, "that which is believed" — the object of faith *(fides quae creditur)* — was expressed with the aid of formulas which were brief at the outset, and were lengthened bit by bit over time as it became necessary to specify the content of faith and to counter its unorthodox opponents.

29. Thus we see that the confession of faith is as old as the church, for it expresses the faith of its members. The confession of faith legitimizes their participation in the sacraments of baptism and the eucharist. Yet this confession of faith is more than words. When Jesus enjoins his disciples to acknowledge their faith before others so that he can acknowledge it before the Father (Matt. 10:32), the context suggests that it is more about the act of confessing than about the words of a formula. Consequently, the Christian confession of faith should be seen less as a way of reciting truth statements than of proving by one's actions that one lives with and for the One who is Truth and Life. By way

---

6. Indeed, the Septuagint translates the Hebrew *qahal YHWH,* "people of God," as *ekklesia tou Theou,* the "church of God."

of example, the pilgrim Egeria reports that in Jerusalem at the end of the fourth century, before inscribing the names of candidates for baptism in the list of catechumens, the bishop would ask neighbors about their conduct.[7]

30. When they give an account of the hope that is in them and that guides their action, Christians will speak of that which Christ taught, which was handed on by the apostles, and held by the church. This handing on of the content of the faith *(fides quae creditur)* takes place especially during catechesis, the oral explanation of the creed to the catechumen, the handing on of the Symbol *(traditio symboli)*. At the end of their instruction and before being baptized the catechumen would repeat or "give back" the same creed *(redditio symboli)*.

31. The process of catechesis followed by baptism is not, however, the only time that the faith of Christians is expressed in the form of a confession. Early Christian literature, beginning with certain texts which were incorporated into the New Testament, as well as some apocryphal and patristic writings, contains many confessions of faith. Some are directly inspired by the canonical Scriptures, others are a reply to specific questions that arose. From the third century on, theological debates become the occasion for writing confessions of faith, either by private persons who wished to state their theological positions openly, or by the first gatherings of local or provincial councils. The question of official Symbols of faith with binding authority emerges in the conciliar age, beginning from Nicaea.[8]

32. In any case, the church understood itself as having received this witness from the apostles. This is why it calls itself apostolic. This apostolic character means that the church does not place its trust in itself. Its confession of faith is founded on the tradition of the apostles, with primacy of place given to Scripture. This raises, however, the twofold problem concerning the apostolicity of Scripture and that of its inerrancy.[9]

7. "Is this person leading a good life? Does he respect his parents? Is he a drunkard or a boaster?" Egeria, *Journal de voyage* 45, 3; SC 296, p. 307. [English translation: *Egeria's Travels,* trans. John Wilkinson (London: SPCK, 1971), 45, 3, p. 144. Subsequent citations are taken from the English version.]

8. See no. 68 below.

9. Inerrancy is the immunity of Scripture from error, by virtue of its inspiration by God.

33. The establishment of the *canon* of Scripture, that is to say the determination of those books which belong and those which would be excluded, is the result of a long evolution in which the whole Christian people interacted with ecclesial authorities (bishops and councils). The canonical lists of the fourth and fifth centuries are the quasi-culmination of a process which, according to the witness of Irenaeus, began in the second century. Besides theological considerations referring to the content of the texts (their orthodoxy) or evoking the authority of their authors (inspiration), the concrete practice of the church seems to have played a decisive role. Indeed, it was most often a question of the "reception" of the scriptural texts, indicated by the criteria of unanimity, their public character, and liturgical use. While the canon appeared closed in principle in the second century, many variations continued to exist into the fourth and fifth centuries.

34. The Scriptures, even those received as canonical, were written and recopied by human persons. It would be unrealistic to think that these copyists could not commit the slightest error in transcription. Yet, as Papias of Hieropolis observes,[10] their goal was to teach and not to deceive, and thus, though such a risk remains, it is negligible. Because Scripture comes from the tradition of the apostles, it is life sustaining for the church. Irenaeus stresses this in his very surprising exegesis of Genesis:

> But flee to the church, suckle at her breast and be nourished with the Lord's Scriptures. For the church has been planted as a garden *(paradidus)* in this world; therefore says the Spirit of God, "You may freely eat from every tree of the garden," that is, "eat from every Scripture of the Lord, but you shall not eat with a haughty mind, nor touch any heretical discord."[11]

Thus, for the bishop of Lyon, Scripture is at one and the same time that by which Christians affirm their faith and a warning against the seductions and errors of heretics. Tertullian, almost a contemporary of

---

10. Eusebius, *Ecclesiastical History*, vol. 1, III, 39, p. 291.

11. Irenaeus, *CH*, V, 20, p. 628. [English translation: *Against Heresies*, The Ante-Nicene Fathers, vol. 1, ed. A. Robins and J. Donaldson (Buffalo: Christian Literature Publishing, 1885), V, 20, 2, p. 548. Slightly emended. Subsequent citations are taken from the English version.]

Irenaeus, tells us that the Scriptures are instruments *(instrumenta),* means which Christians must know how to use in order to develop a coherent doctrine and a sound teaching.[12] In this way, Scripture comes to be regarded equally as the *expression* of the truth and the *criteria* of truth. This idea is summed up later by Gregory of Nyssa when he writes, "We make the Scriptures the rule and the measure of our dogmas. We only approve that which is in accord with the intention of these writings."[13]

3. Three Witnesses on Doctrinal Authority: Irenaeus, Tertullian, Origen

Irenaeus (ca. 130-140 to ca. 202)

35. Irenaeus faced the widespread phenomenon of gnosis and Gnosticism[14] which exercised a dangerous influence within Christian communities. It is important to note the way in which he deals with this important doctrinal and pastoral problem. First, he makes reference to reason, demonstrating the lack of coherence in the philosophical and theological systems of the Gnostics. Second, he appeals to faith, arguing at once from the witness of Scripture and the rule of faith or rule of truth which is unanimously respected in the church. On these two grounds, he introduces a doctrine of the tradition of faith which he juxtaposes with the Gnostic tradition.

36. The work of Irenaeus against the Gnostics is typical of the development of "orthodoxy" in the second century. On one hand, a "champion of the faith" intervenes. Following his example, other champions, especially Origen and Hippolytus, would join in the battle. Their interventions would derive their authority from the very reception accorded them by the churches.

---

12. See Tertullian, *De la prescription contre les hérétiques,* 38, 2-3; SC 46, p. 140. [English translation: *On Prescription Against Heretics,* The Ante-Nicene Fathers, vol. 3, ed. A. Robins and J. Donaldson (Buffalo: Christian Literature Publishing, 1885), 38, pp. 261-262.]

13. Gregory of Nyssa, *Dialogue de l'âme; PG* 46, 49 C. [English translation: *On the Soul and the Resurrection,* in Nicene and Post-Nicene Fathers, Second Series, vol. 5 (Oxford: Parker/New York: Christian Literature Co., 1893), pp. 428-468.]

14. Gnosis or Gnosticism was a widely held belief in Jewish, Greek, and Christian circles. It professed the salvation of an elite group of humanity due to the possession of spiritual knowledge. Gnosticism held a very pessimistic view of the world and of the human body.

On the other hand, there is a dialectic at work between heterodoxy and orthodoxy. The rise of heterodox movements leads the orthodox to clarify and make explicit the meaning of Christian faith. At the same time, this activity by orthodox believers leads to a sharper description of the heterodox position. Today, some people readily accuse the orthodox party of carrying out a process of exclusion. One can only regret the polemical climate of these diverse conflicts. Yet what occurred in this period was a necessary clarification of the content and the parameters of the faith itself. If in fact there was exclusion, it was mutual.

37. The main question of concern for Irenaeus — where he argues from the Scripture in reply to the Gnostics — was that of knowing where to find the truth of the gospel. His response was as follows: the truth of the gospel is to be found in the churches that remain in the tradition of the apostles thanks to the public succession of episkopoi/presbyters to whom the apostles entrusted the churches from the beginning. These churches preserve the Scriptures and interpret them according to the rule of faith.[15]

While Rome, the church of Peter and Paul, has an important role to play, it does not enjoy a monopoly on the truth. Smyrna and Ephesus are also mentioned as trustworthy witnesses to the tradition of the apostles.[16]

38. Whenever he treats this topic, Irenaeus likes to emphasize the three marks of the apostolic succession — "guaranteed" by the presbyter-bishops — which one must look for in the churches:

- The legitimate succession of the episcopate beginning from the apostles.[17]
- But also, "the sure charism of truth according to the good pleasure of God"; or "a holy word"; or "unadulterated and incorrupt speech" or again "an immutable preservation of the Scripture, implying three things: a very complete system of doctrine, and neither receiving addition nor [suffering] curtailment . . . reading [the Word of God] without falsification, and a lawful and diligent exposition in harmony with the Scriptures, but without danger of blasphemy";
- Lastly, "irreproachable conduct"; "an unassailable integrity of conduct"; "the preeminent gift of love."

15. Irenaeus, *Against Heresies,* III, 1-4, pp. 414-417.
16. Irenaeus, *Against Heresies,* III, 3, 4, p. 416.
17. Irenaeus, *Against Heresies,* IV, 26, 2,4, pp. 497-498, and 5; 33, 8, p. 508.

8

These three marks prohibit us from thinking of the church's magisterium as a kind of perfectly functioning mechanism, and hold together its characteristics of both human frailty and faithfulness to the gospel.[18]

39. That being said, what is essential for Irenaeus and is affirmed from the outset of his long discourse on the Scriptures, is that the whole church has received the "gift of God"; "For this gift of God has been entrusted to the church . . . that all the members receiving it may be vivified, and the means of communion with Christ has been distributed throughout it, that is, in the Holy Spirit, the earnest of incorruption, the means of confirming our faith, and the ladder of the ascent to God. . . . For where the church is, there is the Spirit of God, and where the Spirit of God is, there is the church, and every kind of grace."[19]

40. The apostolic succession of presbyter-bishops is not the last word on the question. A long passage attributes the correct interpretation of the Scriptures to the spiritual disciple, who reads the Scripture in the company of a mysterious "presbyter." This passage concerning the spiritual disciple who judges all and is judged by no one illustrates the indwelling of the ecclesial magisterium in the heart of the Christian.[20]

41. Just as the barbarian who is unable to read Scripture possesses their meaning in his heart by the Spirit, the spiritual disciple has something like the equivalent of the sure charism of truth which has graced the magisterium. Does not the relationship of baptismal faith to the Holy Spirit confer upon him that true knowledge, that sort of discernment of the meaning of the scriptures, which are also entirely spiritual?[21]

Without accusing Irenaeus of Platonism or attributing to him a spiritual temperament like that of Newman, it would seem that the bishop of Lyon includes among those charisms inherent in baptismal faith this knowledge or authentic "gnosis" which allows the Christian to legitimately interpret the Scriptures and come near to God through love.[22]

---

18. The three marks were noted in the previous document of the Groupe des Dombes, *Pour une réconciliation des ministères* (Taizé: Les Presses de Taizé, 1973). [English translation: "Towards a Reconciliation of Ministries," in *Modern Ecumenical Agreements on the Ministry,* ed. H. R. McAdoo, trans. Pamela Gaughan (London: SPCK, 1975), pp. 87-107. See no. 13.]

19. Irenaeus, *Against Heresies,* III, 24, 1, p. 458, with reference to 1 Cor. 2:15.

20. Irenaeus, *Against Heresies,* IV, 33, 1-8, pp. 506-508.

21. Irenaeus, *Against Heresies,* III, 4, 2, p. 417; IV, 26, 2, p. 497; IV, 33, 8, p. 508; II, 28, 3, pp. 399-400.

22. Irenaeus, *Against Heresies,* IV, 33, 8, p. 508; II, 26, 1, p. 397.

42. During the quarrel over the date of Easter, Irenaeus demonstrates the responsibility of a brother bishop toward Pope Victor, when the latter is tempted to excommunicate the churches of Asia who follow a different calendar. Irenaeus recalls the primacy of the value of communion to the authoritarian pope, and the secondary importance of a requirement for liturgical uniformity: "The disagreement in the fast confirms our agreement in the faith."[23]

Tertullian (ca. 155–ca. 220)

43. At the very end of the second century, Tertullian, in his treatise, *The Prescription Against the Heretics,* asks when and by what intermediary we have received the doctrine which makes us Christian. Christ, he explains, conferred on the apostles the mission to preach what he revealed to them. They carried out this mission by establishing churches and entrusting the churches with that same mission. So much so, that it would be on the basis of the faith preached in the churches that one could discern true doctrine from those that were false. These early churches were apostolic because they were one, something we can see in the fact that their teaching was founded on the common reading of the apostolic writings, and in their mutual expression of fraternity and charity.

44. Unlike the apostolic churches which draw the rule of faith from the Scriptures handed down by the apostles, as they were read and understood in the church, heretics based their false doctrines on the falsification of the Scriptures. Tertullian inveighs against three principal leaders of the heterodox movements: "By what right, Marcion, do you hew my wood? By whose permission, Valentinus, are you diverting the streams of my fountain? By what power, Appelles, are you removing my landmarks?"[24] Thus, he indicates the ways in which they falsify the scriptures and how this leads to teaching a doctrine which is not that of the church of Christ. Like Marcion, one can amputate the scriptures, selecting only what one finds agreeable. Like Valentinus, one can adapt the scriptures to whatever is in fashion or to what one wants to say. Or like Appelles, one can add new revelations to corroborate one's claims.

Origen (ca. 185-253)

45. In the early part of the third century, Origen was aware that many Christians disagreed on questions that were sometimes of major importance. Thus,

---

23. In Eusebius, *Ecclesiastical History,* V, 24, 13, p. 511.
24. Tertullian, "The Prescription Against Heretics," 37, p. 261.

in his treatise *On First Principles,* he proposes a distinction that would help to resolve doctrinal disagreements.

46. First, he recalls a number of points that were clearly recognized in the preaching of the apostles (for example, the affirmation that God is the Creator of the universe or that his Son became man). It is therefore necessary to remain faithful to this preaching, "the teaching of the church, handed down in . . . succession from the apostles to the present day; we maintain that that only is to be believed as the truth which in no way conflicts with the tradition of the church and of the apostles."[25]

47. Nonetheless, continues Origen, the apostles did not hand down "the grounds for their statements," "they left [them] to be investigated by such as merit the higher gifts of the Spirit and in particular by such as should afterward receive through the Holy Spirit himself the graces of language, wisdom and knowledge." The determination of that which belongs to the object of faith thus opens the way, paradoxically, for theological research. The apostles did not speak on all things "to supply the more diligent of those who came after them, such as should prove to be lovers of wisdom, with an exercise in which to display the fruit of their ability."[26] Thus, things which have not yet been decided, "we must investigate to the best of our power from Holy Scripture, inquiring with wisdom and diligence."[27] In the end it is a matter of creating "a single body of doctrine, with the aid of such illustrations and declarations as he shall find in the Holy Scriptures and of such conclusions as he shall ascertain to follow logically from them when rightly understood."[28]

48. This distinction between that which is necessary as the object of faith and that which remains an object of free research by the theologian is undoubtedly an important principle of discernment in doctrinal debates. Origen himself applies this principle in his treatise, as he does not hesitate to offer his own opinions freely on points that had not been decided by the church. Of course, in the years that followed a number of his opinions earned him a reputation as a "heretic." Yet it is only fair to say that, during his lifetime, the church had not yet pronounced itself on the questions at issue.

49. Elsewhere, the "Dialogue of Origen with Heraclides" demonstrates in a remarkable way how a doctrinal conflict with a bishop sus-

25. Origène, *Traité des principes,* Préf., 2; SC 252, p. 79. [English translation: *Origen on First Principles,* ed. G. W. Butterworth (London: SPCK, 1936), Book I, Preface 3, p. 2.]

26. *Origen on First Principles,* Pref. 3, p. 2.

27. *Origen on First Principles,* Pref. 4, p. 2.

28. *Origen on First Principles,* Pref. 10, p. 6.

pected of heterodoxy was treated in the period 244-249. The controversy, which probably began in Arabia, centered on a debate concerning the eucharistic prayer. The Bishop Heraclides gave the impression of failing to maintain an adequate distinction between the Father and the Son. An episcopal meeting was called. The bishops presented their points of view. Heraclides made a profession of faith. Then Origen, who had been invited to the meeting, entered into a discussion with Heraclides. While speaking along the same lines as Heraclides in affirming the divinity of the Son, Origen tried to get him to acknowledge the Son's distinct personality from that of the Father.[29]

50. This episode had a great impact, especially since it took place not only in the presence of bishops. Origen required that the priests and the faithful who were present offer their solemn adherence to the specific decisions of the assembly.[30] Though it was, of course, a regional assembly, Origen did not hesitate to say "The whole church is here listening. It is not fitting for doctrinal differences to exist from church to church."[31] If the bishops had a role in this debate, the magisterium was undeniably represented here by Origen, a simple priest, in his capacity as an expert in the assembly. He is the one they consulted, and it is he that, with as much humility as mastery, led the discussion and established the doctrine. And the church, including the bishops, bowed to his arguments.[32]

51. Apart from the witness of Irenaeus, Tertullian, and Origen, we wish to emphasize, at the conclusion of this section, that throughout the second and third centuries there were a number of consultations among bishops or Christian communities.[33] By means of such consul-

---

29. Entretien d'Origène avec Héraclide, 1 and 2; SC 67, pp. 53-59. J. Scherer notes, the "spirit of understanding, trust, and Christian charity that characterized these debates [l'esprit de compréhension, confiance, et de charité chrétienne qui anima ces débats]," SC 67, p. 23. [English translation: Origen on First Principles, "Dialogue of Origen with Heraclides and His Fellow Bishops on the Father and the Son, and the Soul," trans. Robert J. Daly in Ancient Christian Writers, vol. 54 (New York: Paulist, 1992), pp. 57-59.]

30. "Dialogue of Origen with Heraclides," 4 and 5, pp. 60-62.

31. "Dialogue of Origen with Heraclides," 1, pp. 57-58.

32. This is not an isolated episode in Origen's life. He took part in other discussions of this sort, notably at the Synod of Bostra with Bishop Berylle, who held a heretical position, and whom he succeeded in leading to a more orthodox opinion (see Eusebius, Ecclesiastical History, VI, 33, 1-3, pp. 87-89).

33. See Groupe des Dombes, Le ministère de communion dans l'Église universelle (Paris: Centurion, 1986), no. 19.

tations, which often emerged on an occasional basis before they became more regular, the churches attempted to overcome problems connected to the diversity of traditions and to divergences in doctrine. From local gatherings to regional synods (synods whose authority bound every particular bishop), they demonstrated their concern to restore or to consolidate their communion in faith. Such consultations were already preparing the way for the great councils of the East which, beginning from the fourth century, would play a major role in the exercise of doctrinal authority.

II. The Great Councils in the East and Their Theology

1. The Council of Nicaea (325)

52. The meeting of the first ecumenical council at Nicaea in 325, at the behest of Constantine, was something new in the life of the church.[34] The fathers gathered at Nicaea were conscious that this meeting differed from the preceding councils and synods. It brought together bishops of East and West. Participants referred to it as the "great and holy council," using a new expression. Its disciplinary decisions were binding on vast territories. It produced canons that applied to the universal church. In the field of doctrine, the fathers were likewise aware of the definitive and irreformable character of their decision to add new expressions to the Symbol of faith.

53. Nonetheless, the theology of the ecumenical council did not exist prior to the gathering of the Council of Nicaea. We know this from the fifty years of bitter debate in the East concerning its decisions and from the number of councils — some of which claimed to be ecumenical — that modified and at times contradicted the expressions chosen at Nicaea. These debates were brought to a close by the reconciliation of 381 at the Council of Constantinople I. At that time, the Council of Nicaea was "received" in the churches and its authority was recognized.

54. Athanasius of Alexandria (ca. 295-373) played an important role

---

34. It was only relatively new, in as much as it had been preceded by the early tradition of local and regional councils.

in this process of reception. It is interesting to note the evolution in his conception of conciliar authority, reflected in expressions such as, "eternal [boundary stones] which the fathers placed," and "the word of the Lord which came through the ecumenical Synod at Nicaea, abides forever."[35] Elsewhere he says, "The whole inhabited earth (the *oikumene*) gave its consent to the faith of Nicaea."[36]

55. The development of a theological doctrine concerning the meeting of an ecumenical council is therefore the consequence of the lived experience of the churches and resulted in the definitive reception of the teaching of Nicaea. It was the *actual authority* of the council which gave rise to a doctrine of its *canonical authority*. Thus, the authority of a council does not function automatically. A certain number of conditions must be met before a conciliar gathering is considered legitimate and authoritative. Among these conditions, the phenomenon of *reception* is essential. A council can never be considered apart from the process of reception to which it gives rise, that is to say, the fact that a whole group of ecclesial communities with their bishops recognize its teaching as an expression of the apostolic faith.

56. The lesson to be learned concerning the authority of a council can be summed up as follows: An ecumenical council which brings together the bishops, successors of the apostles who preside over all the churches, is assisted by the Holy Spirit to take only those decisions which are in conformity with the faith of the apostles. For the unanimity of the churches is expressed in its teaching. For this reason every council is a "new assembly of Jerusalem." According to this definition of a council, one must consider its celebration a unique event and include the phenomenon of its reception.

2. Ephesus (431), the Act of Union (433), and Chalcedon (451)

57. We ought not to forget the trials and tribulations that went along with the unfolding of the ecumenical councils when we consider their doctrinal authority. The first problem raised by the meeting of the

---

35. Athanase, *Epître aux Africains;* PG 26, 1032 A; 1048 A. [English translation: Athanasius, "Synodal Letter *(ad Afros),*" Nicene and Post-Nicene Fathers, Second Series, vol. 4 (Oxford: Parker/New York: Christian Literature Co., 1892), pp. 489-495.]

36. Athanasius, "Synodal Letter *(ad Afros),*" p. 489.

Council of Ephesus was how to know which council was true. Indeed, two rival councils were held at Ephesus in June of 431: the council opened by Cyril of Alexandria prior to the arrival of the Antiochene bishops, which condemned Nestorius and acclaimed the first letter of Cyril to Nestorius; and the council held immediately afterward by John of Antioch, which excommunicated Cyril. Which one was a legitimate meeting and manifested the authenticity of faith?

58. In this situation of conflict, the authority of the Council of Ephesus remained open to question. All parties recognized the need to move beyond this impasse. A new development took place, which must be seen in relation to the conciliar event. This was the Act of Union concluded between John of Antioch and Cyril of Alexandria in 433. In a spirit of both human and doctrinal reconciliation, Cyril of Alexandria recognized the legitimacy of the Antiochene christological language, using a formula that would give birth to the future definition of Chalcedon, whereas John of Antioch broke ranks with Nestorius by confessing Mary as "Mother of God" *(theotokos)*. Two christological languages, that of Alexandria and that of Antioch, mutually recognized each other and respected their differences. Though unanimity was not attained, the ecumenicity of doctrinal decisions was achieved.

59. The public character of a council, even when legitimately convened, is not sufficient to establish its doctrinal authority. These meetings must not only respect people's rights, they must acknowledge the legitimacy of complementary points of view. The meeting of the Second Council of Ephesus in 449, under the passionate direction of Dioscorus of Alexandria, gave rise to violence and assaults against Flavian of Constantinople. There was such a partisan spirit at work in favor of the Monophysite position, that the doctrinal letter sent to Flavian by Pope Leo could not be heard. The council was never "received" in either the East or the West.

60. Pope Leo the Great would write of this gathering, "It is not a council, but a Robber Synod *(non concilium, sed latrocinium)* held in an uproar and for reasons of secular hatred." He refused, together with the Roman synod, to consider it a council. The position was in agreement with that of the East. But it illustrates the delicate problem of the relationship between the pope and the council. The practice would develop of considering that a council could only be considered authoritative when approved or confirmed by the pope. In later times the bishops of Rome would firmly uphold this prerogative. Must one see in Leo's attitude the refusal of a juridical "confirmation"?

61. There is no indication that Pope Sylvester confirmed the Council of Nicaea, at which his legates presided. There was no question of any confirmation of the Council of Constantinople I, since this council of the Eastern bishops was not ecumenical in the same sense as Nicaea. Its Symbol was subsequently recognized by Chalcedon, giving it a sort of retroactive ecumenical status.

62. The question is raised for the first time at the first Council of Ephesus. The legates of the pope read the letter of Celestine at this gathering, and it was acclaimed by the fathers and "received." Yet there remains a basic ambiguity with regard to the meaning of this "reception." The legates seemed to think that the council sided with the doctrine of Celestine. Thus, the priest Phillip would say, "The members were joined to the head." But the council fathers considered that they had simply recognized that the pope was in agreement with their own decisions. On the other hand, it is not possible to speak of a formal "confirmation" of the council by Celestine, even if he expressed his agreement with its decisions. It would be anachronistic to speak of a confirmation in the modern sense of the word, to describe what took place in this period.

63. As for the attitude of Leo following the council of 449, this cannot be viewed as a juridical decision for annulment. He makes the simple observation that the "Robber Synod" cannot be taken for a council, since the voice of the West was not heard there.

64. The fallout from the Council of Ephesus raised a new and formidable question. This council is the origin of the first enduring schism among churches. Certain Eastern bishops would refuse to accept the Act of Union and joined together with the Syrian Church of Persia which, in 486, officially adopted a Nestorian doctrine. Thus, a Nestorian church continued to live on the margins of the Byzantine Empire. The Assyrian Church of the East continues to exist in our day. Its catholicos, Patriarch Mar Dinkha IV, has asked that it no longer be called "Nestorian," given the pejorative connotation of this adjective.

65. The Patriarch Mar Dinkha IV signed a "Common Christological Declaration" together with Pope John Paul II on November 11, 1994. The language of this text is closer to that of the Act of Union and the definition of Chalcedon than to the language of Ephesus. This document clearly expresses our faith in the incarnation of the Son of God in the womb of the Virgin Mary. The ancient and disputed formula "Mother of God" *(theotokos)* gives rise to two types of expressions:

"Mary, Mother of Christ our God and Savior" on the Assyrian side, and "Mother of God" and "Mother of Christ" on the Catholic side.[37]

66. This contemporary event of doctrinal reconciliation on christological matters contributes a new and important teaching: the quarrels of the past often centered on questions of language. Unanimity in the language of faith seemed necessary for the communion of faith. The distance of time has allowed us to better understand the relationship between the language and the content of faith. The principle that prevailed in the 1994 agreement consists in recognizing the possibility of a real agreement in faith expressed in different language. It goes beyond what the early councils had recognized.

67. We will only mention the Council of Chalcedon (451) briefly, for from the perspective of the functioning of conciliar authority, it merely serves to confirm what we have learned from Nicaea and Ephesus. Let us note simply that it was the Council of Chalcedon that "received" the Symbol of Constantinople I, and in this way recognized the ecumenical character of this council. Qualitatively, this presents an original phenomenon of reception. Yet, while Chalcedon "received" Constantinople I, the reception of its own teachings proved a very difficult process. Partisans of the "two natures of Christ" opposed the partisans of "one single nature" (or *Monophysites*). The difficult reception of Chalcedon, as we shall see, became the occasion for the gathering of the Council of Constantinople II.

3. The Recognized Authority of the Creed

68. In response to the trinitarian and christological quarrels of the fourth and fifth centuries, the bishops gathered in the ecumenical councils to draw up the confessions of faith. In this way the confession of faith — the free and joyful proclamation of what is at the heart of the gospel — gradually comes to be regarded as a criterion or test of orthodoxy. This is what is meant by the ban against any abrogation of the creed by the first canon of Constantinople I, a council which had itself developed and modified the creed! The Monophysite and bishop of

---

37. "Common Christological Declaration between the Catholic Church and the Assyrian Church of the East," in *Growth in Agreement II*, ed. Jeffrey Gros, Harding Meyer, and William G. Rusch (Geneva: WCC/Grand Rapids: Eerdmans, 2000), pp. 711-712.

Antioch, Peter the Fuller, was the first to include the Credo in the liturgy of his church in the second half of the fifth century. In using the Creed of Nicaea-Constantinople in this way, he wished to emphasize that it was the only true Credo of the church, in contrast to the definition of Chalcedon which he condemned.

4. The Crisis of Constantinople II (553)

69. The context prior to the meeting of the Council of Constantinople II was characterized by an extremely complex disagreement between the Emperor Justinian, Pope Vigilius, and the bishops of East and West. Justinian wished to bring about a reconciliation of the Monophysites, partisans of Severus of Antioch, with those who held the position of two natures, partisans of Chalcedon. To achieve this end he took sides and condemned the writings of three Antiochene authors who were already deceased by this time: Theodore of Mopsuestia, Theodoret of Cyrus, and Ibas of Edessa. This was a measure of compromise intended to preserve the authority of Chalcedon, while at the same time giving unconditional support to the formulas of Cyril of Alexandria. This edict of condemnation came to be known as the "Three Chapters." It gave rise to interminable debates from the conference of 532 until the meeting of the Council of Constantinople II in 553, and to further controversies in the West. Although Justinian was able to convince the bishops of the East that his edict of condemnation was well founded, he failed to convince Pope Vigilius and the bishops of the West, some of whom did not hesitate to break away in schism.

70. In these debates we see a clash among three instances of doctrinal authority: the emperor, the bishops — divided among themselves, and the pope. None of their claims to institutional authority is clearly defined or undisputed. In particular, the recognized authority of the bishop of Rome remains subject to uncertainty in the eyes of the emperor and the council fathers. In any case, no single authority is recognized a priori during these debates as a guarantor of orthodoxy. It is rather the orthodoxy of faith that confers institutional authority on the council or the pope, as each partner identifies themselves spontaneously with orthodoxy.[38]

71. The council took place in a climate of tension and extreme violence be-

38. On this very complex issue, see Claire Sotinel, "Le concile, l'empereur, l'évêque. Les statuts d'autorité dans le débat sur les trois chapitres," in *Orthodoxie — Christianisme — Histoire,* ed. S. Elm, E. Rebillard, and A. Romano (École française de Rome, 2000), pp. 275-299.

tween the Emperor Justinian and Pope Vigilius. For the primary objective of the emperor was to have the council ratify the condemnation of the *Three Chapters,* whereas, the pope refused to condemn the memory of men who had died in communion with the church. The violence of the emperor toward the pope and the imperial pressure exerted over the bishops led to such a conflict between the pope and the council that one might ask whether the council was truly free and valid.

72. The work of the council was summed up in two documents: a long polemical sentence against the *Three Chapters,* and a series of fourteen doctrinal canons. The first ten canons constitute an interpretation of the definition of Chalcedon emphasizing the agreement of the council with the affirmations of Ephesus. The last four canons repeat the condemnation of Origen and of the authors of the *Three Chapters.*

73. The first problem raised by this council comes from the fact that it anathematized Pope Vigilius and held most of its sessions in a break from communion with him. It even upheld a "conciliarist" thesis, affirming the superiority of a council over the pope. The second problem comes from the reversal of the pope's position, under pressure from Justinian. First Vigilius resisted by a decision *(Constitutum)* that he declared to be irrevocable; then he finally gave in and confirmed the work of the council concerning the *Three Chapters.*

74. Paradoxically, the council was "confirmed" by successive popes, including Vigilius, Pelagius I, and Gregory the Great, on the question of the *Three Chapters,* but its christological canons were not. Nonetheless, the distance of history allows us to appreciate that the confirmation of the *Three Chapters* affair fell into complete disuse, while the christological canons came to be received as an act of interpreting the Council of Chalcedon. This paradox reveals how the fruitfulness of the council greatly surpasses the immediate intention of its actors through the phenomenon of reception.

75. What emerges from this review of events confirms the teaching already given by the Council of Ephesus. A council can meet amid the infinite vicissitudes of life in which one would search in vain to know who represents the ultimate juridical instance of authority. It was only in the slow unfolding over time in the life of the church, through the phenomenon of reception, that we discerned the definitive authority of this council.

5. Constantinople III (680-681) and the Case of Honorius

76. At the instigation of the Emperor Justinian, the fifth ecumenical council condemned what were called the *Three Chapters*. The Monophysites remained less than satisfied in spite of these condemnations. Patriarch Sergius of Constantinople therefore proposed a compromise. In order to avoid the controverted question — are there one or two natures in the incarnation of Christ? — he wrote of a single activity *(energeia)* in Christ *(monoenergism)*. In 634 Pope Honorius I (625-638) approved of his explanations. However, in that same year the patriarch of Jerusalem, Sophronius, confessed to two activities in Jesus Christ in his letter of enthronement. This was the cause of renewed agitation among the Monophysites, partisans of a single nature, and the Chalcedonians, who upheld the two natures of Christ. The Emperor Heraclitus asked Patriarch Sergius to find a new compromise and he in turn proposed that one only speak of a single will in Christ. Heraclitus imposed this position, which came to be called Monothelitism, by decree in 638.

77. It wasn't long before opposition appeared to this Christology imposed by law, but it was repressed. Thus, Pope Martin I, whose synod gathered at Rome to condemn Monothelitism, was deported to Crimea where he died. In the same way, Maximus the Confessor, the great anti-Monothelite theologian, died in 662 after suffering severe torture.

In order to restore order, the Emperor Constantine IV Pogonat called what would become the sixth ecumenical council. Pope Agatho gave his consent. The council met at Constantinople in the room of the cupola (*Troullos* in Greek; hence the name *in Trullo*) of the Sacred Palace from November 7, 680, to September 16 of the following year. The definition *(horos)* of the Council of Constantinople III confesses two wills in Jesus Christ, one human and one divine. The council declared anathema among others, all those who subscribed to the affirmations of Patriarch Sergius which it condemned. Among those condemned was Pope Honorius I, "banished from the holy church."

78. The Council of Constantinople III raised a new problem, that of a "heretical" pope. Its condemnation failed to provoke a protest from either the Roman legates or Pope Leo II, who confirmed it as the sixth ecumenical council. Its condemnations would be repeated in 692 by the Quinisext Council of Constantinople and in 787 by the Council of Nicaea II.

79. The real problem lies elsewhere. Whatever the effective error of Honorius, several councils, popes, and the whole of Christianity consider him a heretic. What is the significance of such a judgment for our

understanding of the relationship between a pope and a council on one hand, and of papal infallibility on the other? The worrisome question of the heretical pope will return toward the end of the Middle Ages and will generate an immense body of literature. Some will claim that the condemnation of Constantinople was mistaken (A. Pighi). An appeasing and conciliatory interpretation would regard Honorius's error as a private and personal mistake which did not bind the see of Rome (Nicholas of Cusa). But Reformed theologians, Gallicans (for example, Bossuet), and Jansenists held, on the contrary, that that the pope's heresy was committed by a "public Doctor."

80. The development of these various positions continues right up to the debate that took place at Vatican I in 1869, and included references to the cases of Popes Liberius[39] and Vigilius. The case of Vigilius, who was condemned by an ecumenical council, proved a thorny one, and the anti-infallibilists did not hesitate to cite this example in favor of their position. The case of Honorius served as the very example of a heretical pope throughout history.[40] However, the council would not mention it, reasoning that Honorius did not teach Monoenergism *ex cathedra*, but that he had merely approved the assertions of Patriarch Sergius in private correspondence. Thus, he simply expressed his personal view, and was not speaking in the name of the whole church.

6. The Emergence of the Pope's Doctrinal Authority

81. The age of the first ecumenical councils reveals a specific relationship between the pope and a council. Even if the council were called by the emperor, it would not take place without the agreement of the pope. His legates would normally take part. The acts of the councils gradually came to be confirmed by the pope, as he contributed to the phenomenon of its reception. At times, the popes withheld their consent from some canon or another, as did Leo in the case of canon 28 from the Council of Chalcedon. For their part, the councils listened to

39. Pope Liberius (352-366) was never condemned, yet his case was analogous, for he ceded for a time to pressure from the Arians and accepted the very ambiguous formula of the Council of Sirmium (357).

40. See G. Kreuzer, *Die Honoriusfrage im Mittelalter und Neuzeit* (Stuttgart: Hiersemann, 1975).

and received the voice of the pope. All of this reflects the special authority of the pope in relation to the councils, an authority that increased over time.

82. The problem of whether the authority of a council is greater than that of the pope, or whether the authority of the pope is greater than that of a council, was never clearly resolved. Opinions on this question were markedly different in the East, gravitating spontaneously toward the former interpretation, whereas the West quickly adopted the latter position.

83. In 343 the Council of Sardica made an interesting contribution to the churches' understanding of the pope's role. If a bishop considered that a case had not been judged in his favor at the local or regional level, he would appeal to the see of Rome. The pope would, if he considered it necessary, annul the local decision. Yet he would never proceed to judge the appeal himself. He would refer the case to a regional jurisdiction other than the one who had first decided the case. Thus, the role of the see of Rome was to function as a "court of annulment."

III. Doctrinal Authority in the West after Nicaea

1. Augustine (354-430)

84. For Latin Christianity the work of Augustine stands as an important source of reflection on doctrinal authority in the church. This authority remains above all subordinated to divine authority, revealed in a unique and exemplary way in the authority of Christ. The authority of Christ is itself perpetuated in the authority of Holy Scripture. Augustine underlines the primacy of the authority of Scripture in relation to the books of later writers: the authority of the Old and New Testaments "has come down to us from the apostles through the succession of bishops and the extension of the church, and from a position of lofty supremacy, claims the submission of every faithful and pious mind."[41] It was against this background that Augustine was led to de-

---

41. Augustin, *Contra Fauste,* XI, 5; éd. Vivès, XXV, p. 539. [English translation: *Against Faustus,* Nicene and Post-Nicene Fathers, First Series, vol. 4: *Saint Augustine: The Writings Against the Manicheans and Against the Donatists* (Grand Rapids: Eerdmans, 1956), p. 180.]

clare himself on the matter of doctrinal authority, notably, during the controversies against the Donatists and the Pelagians.

85. In *De baptismo* (ca. 400) Augustine replied to the Donatists, who based themselves on the authority of Cyprian in refusing the validity of baptism administered by dissidents, by appealing to the continuity of liturgical custom and of the "council of the whole" that had decided the question after the age of Cyprian: "confirmed by the antiquity of the custom itself, and by the subsequent authority of a plenary council."[42] Augustine certainly attaches great value to the moral authority of Cyprian. However, in his view, Cyprian's argument concerning the baptism of heretics cannot be granted the same value as the doctrinal judgment of a council of the universal church. Moreover, even though Cyprian considered the baptism of heretics to be null, he did not wish to break communion with those Christians who thought otherwise. Because the church had not yet pronounced itself on this point, he placed the peace of the church above his personal convictions. It was precisely this attitude that Augustine exhorted the Donatists to imitate: "Cease, therefore, to bring forward against us the authority of Cyprian in favor of repeating baptism, but cling with us to the example of Cyprian for the preservation of unity."[43]

86. While Augustine does not follow Cyprian on the matter of the baptism of heretics, he appeals to his authority to defend the doctrine of original sin. He refers to Cyprian's authority in his first writings against Pelagius (412) and emphasizes the fact that Cyprian based his position on "the decree of a council."[44] He also refers to the authority of Jerome, yet he appeals even more to a unanimous consensus on the doctrine of original sin — a doctrine that was above all founded on the testimony of Holy Scripture.[45] Later, taking as a pretext the praise conferred on Ambrose of Milan by Pelagius, Augustine cites passages from Ambrose to support his theology of grace. At the same time, he re-

---

42. Augustin, *Sur le baptême,* IV, 6,9; *BA* 29, p. 255. This is probably a reference to the Council of Arles (314). [English translation: Augustine, *On Baptism,* Nicene and Post-Nicene Fathers, First Series, vol. 4, 6-9, p. 450.]

43. Augustine, *On Baptism,* 7, 12, p. 430.

44. Augustin, *Sur la peine et la rémission des péchés,* III, 5, 11; éd. Vivès, XXX, p. 112. [English translation: *On the Merits and Remission of Sins, and on the Baptism of Infants,* Nicene and Post-Nicene Fathers, vol. 5: *Saint Augustine's Anti-Pelagian Work,* ed. Philip Shaff (Grand Rapids: Eerdmans, 1956), III, 11, p. 73.]

45. Augustine, *On the Merits and Remission of Sins,* III, 12, p. 73.

calls that Ambrose himself, "however holy and learned he is, he is not to be compared to the authority of the canonical Scriptures."[46] References to Cyprian and to Ambrose appear again in the writings against Julian of Eclanum. Here again Augustine takes care to note the limitations of this "patristic argument." However real, the authority of those who have commented upon the Scriptures can never equal the authority of the Scriptures themselves.[47] What counts, after all, is not so much the testimony of these few authors as the uninterrupted witness of a faith that is "true, truly Christian, and authentic, handed on in the Sacred Scriptures from ancient times, maintained and preserved by our ancestors until our present age when these people have attempted to shake it." This same faith "will hereafter by God's good will be retained and kept."[48]

87. The burden of such witness is especially incumbent on the bishops who, Augustine emphasizes, bear a common responsibility in matters of doctrine. This last point is even more remarkable given that, during the Pelagian controversy, episcopal communion was broken more than once. During the Council of Diospolis (415) the bishops of Palestine declared the doctrine of Pelagius to be catholic. The bishops of North Africa reacted by condemning Pelagius and his disciple Celestius in a council of their own (416). Augustine was nonetheless able to establish that although the bishops of Palestine had acted out of charity toward Pelagius, they too had essentially rejected his doctrine. The two colleges of bishops were thus in full communion of faith. A new crisis arose in 417 with the rehabilitation, at least provisionally, of Celestius and Pelagius by Pope Zosimus. Here again, Augustine demonstrated that the pope had acted from a purely pastoral

---

46. *La grâce du Christ et le péché originel,* I, 43, 47; *BA* 22, p. 141. [English translation: *On the Grace of Christ, and On Original Sin,* Nicene and Post-Nicene Fathers, vol. 5, I, 47, p. 233.]

47. See especially *Réponse à deux lettres de pélagiens,* IV, 8, 21 to IV, 12, 34; *BA* 23, pp. 601-657. Augustine also refers to a text of Ambrosiaster, which he erroneously attributes to Hilary, ibid., IV, 4, 7; p. 567. [English translation: *Against Two Letters of the Pelagians,* Nicene and Post-Nicene Fathers, vol. 5, IV, 21, pp. 425-426; and IV, 7, p. 420.]

48. Augustine, *Against Two Letters of the Pelagians,* IV, 32, p. 433. See also *Against Julian,* where Augustine refers at length to the Fathers that went before him: Irenaeus, Hilary, Ambrose, Gregory of Nyzianzus, Basil, John Chrysostom, and other bishops of both West and East. The unanimity of the Fathers weighs more in his argument than the testimony of any individual author. *Saint Augustine Against Julian,* The Fathers of the Church: A New Translation, vol. 35 (New York: Fathers of the Church, 1957), I, 3, 5–I, 7, 35, pp. 7-43, and II, 2, 4–II, 10, 37, pp. 58-103.

motive, believing, in good faith, that Celestius desired to submit to the orthodox faith. He maintained that Zosimus had always been faithful to the orthodox faith, and that the temporary rehabilitation of these two heretics did not imply any doctrinal disagreement between the apostolic see and the African bishops. Augustine's involvement in the Pelagian controversy thus reveals his strong sense of the co-responsibility of bishops in matters of faith, and the particular importance he gives to the communion of the bishops with Rome. Rome's authority came from the fact that the see of Rome is the see of Peter, in that part of the world "where the Lord chose to crown the first of the apostles by a very glorious martyrdom."[49]

2. Vincent of Lerins († between 435 and 450)

88. A little later, around the year 430, the monk Vincent of Lerins wrote an "aide-memoire" *(commonitorium)* in which he asked, "how, and by what definite, and as it were, universal rule I might distinguish the truth of the catholic faith from the falsity of heretical perversion?" Of course, one might object, "Since the canon of Scripture is complete and is in itself sufficient, what need is there to join it to the authority of ecclesiastical interpretation?" To which Vincent immediately replied, "owing to the depth of the Holy Scripture itself, all do not receive it in one and the same sense." The interpretation of the holy books must therefore be subject to a rule that Vincent formulates as follows: "we take great care that we hold that which has been believed everywhere, always, by all."[50]

89. The "Lerinian canon" implies that the value of a doctrine cannot be dependent upon a single opinion (for example, that of Augustine, some of whose ideas were refused by Vincent!). The authority of a given doctrine is rather related to its universality in space and time, ac-

---

49. Augustine, *Against Julian,* I, 4, 13, pp. 14-15. See also *Against Two letters of the Pelagians,* and the dedication of Augustine to Pope Boniface: "Since the pastoral [ministry of oversight] is common to all of us who discharge the office of the episcopate (although you are preeminent therein and on a loftier height) I do what I can in respect of my small portion of the charge." I, 2, p. 378.

50. Vincent of Lérins, *Communitorium [Aide-mémoire],* 2; trad. M. Meslin (Namur: Du Soleil Levant, 1959), pp. 37-38; [English translation: *The Commonitory of St. Vincent of Lerins,* trans. T. H. Bindley (London: SPCK, 1914), pp. 22-26.]

cording to the three requirements formulated in his canon: the requirement of ecumenicity, for "we confess one faith to be true which the whole church throughout the world confesses";[51] the requirement of antiquity, for "we in no wise depart from those interpretations which it is plain our ancestors and fathers proclaimed";[52] and the requirement of a quasi-general agreement, for "we eagerly follow the definitions and beliefs of all, or certainly nearly all, priests and doctors alike."[53]

90. Vincent of Lerins adds to this statement of the canon two other criteria. On one hand, the criterion of progress in the understanding of faith: dogma is "consolidated" and even "develops" in the course of time, yet in such a way that it remains "uncorrupted and unimpaired, full and perfect in the measurement of its parts."[54] On the other hand, the criterion of reading the Scriptures in conformity with "the traditions of the universal church and the rule of catholic doctrine," according to the threefold requirement for universality, antiquity, and unanimous consent.[55]

91. In modern times, the Lerinian canon has been enlisted by both Catholics and Protestants to support their respective positions — by Catholics to accuse Protestants of rejecting certain articles of faith, and by Protestants to accuse Catholics of unduly adding to the traditional expression of faith. This is an indication that the rule articulated by Vincent of Lerins is not adequate, as it stands, to settle the question of doctrinal authority. The limits of this rule become evident from the moment one attempts to apply it in an absolute way to a given doctrine whose early origin is not attested explicitly, or on which there is no universal agreement, at least for a certain period of time. Nonetheless, it establishes an essential principle that can be formulated negatively: it is not possible to hold as true that which would not be held by some and would not be the object of an ecclesial consensus. Stated positively, the contribution of the canon is revealed in relation to what constitutes the heart of the confession of faith. If it cannot always be followed to the letter, it nonetheless provides a number of criteria that reflect a primary concern for communion in faith and to that end, retain their value as points of reference in the exercise of doctrinal authority.

51. Vincent of Lerins, *Commonitory*, p. 26.
52. Vincent of Lerins, *Commonitory*, p. 26.
53. Vincent of Lerins, *Commonitory*, p. 26. Note that the expression "nearly all" nuances the statement of the rule that, in chapter 2, speaks of a "general agreement" and a "unanimous consent" (p. 26).
54. Vincent of Lerins, *Commonitory*, p. 91.
55. Vincent of Lerins, *Commonitory*, p. 106.

IV. The Role of the Primate and the Patriarchs

92. In the section on the councils of the East we made reference to the relationships which existed among certain churches in the second half of the patristic era. Even though these relationships were at times conflicted, they nonetheless testify to the establishment of regional structures, each of which was genuinely autonomous while at the same time remaining in communion with the universal church. It is important to consider this patriarchal organization which was a feature of both the East and the West, and which had an impact on the exercise of doctrinal authority as well as on the understanding of the primacy recognized as belonging to the bishop of Rome.[56]

93. The term "pentarchy" was given to this form of ecclesial organization which took shape around five major sees in the last centuries of the patristic era. It first centered on the three apostolic sees of Jerusalem, Antioch, and Alexandria, to which Constantinople was added, due to its political importance. These four patriarchal sees had jurisdiction over the churches of their respective regions. The see of Rome, for its part, formed the patriarchate of the West. Indeed, because of its primacy of honor, Rome had always been considered first among the five sees, even though, as patriarchate of the West, it was in a situation analogous to that of the four patriarchates of the East. This organization as a "pentarchy" was recognized by the Council of Constantinople IV: "Therefore we declare that no secular powers should treat with disrespect any of those who hold the office of patriarch or seek to move them from their high positions, but rather they should esteem them as worthy of all honor and reverence. This applies in the first place to the most holy pope of old Rome, secondly to the patriarch of Constantinople, and then to the patriarchs of Alexandria, Antioch, and Jerusalem."[57]

94. According to this system of organization, each of the patriarchal churches, directed by the patriarchs with their synods of bishops, had its own heritage and enjoyed a genuine autonomy in the administration of its respective dioceses. The Church of Rome rarely inter-

---

56. We presented an initial consideration of this question in our document, *Le ministère de communion dans l'Église universelle*, nos. 28 and 29.

57. "Constantinople IV 869-879," in *Decrees of the Ecumenical Councils*, vol. 1, ed. Norman P. Tanner (London: Sheed and Ward/Georgetown: Georgetown University Press, 1990), canon 21, p. 182.

vened in the affairs of other churches except on important matters of faith, and notably, whenever one of them appealed to her as to the highest court. The responsibility of the bishop of Rome in relation to the universal church was therefore distinct from the role he exercised as patriarch of the West. This distinction was made clearly in the case of Pope Gregory the Great (590-604). Indeed, he exercised a primacy over the other patriarchs, for, as bishop of Rome, he presided over the communion of all the churches in faith and charity. Yet it was only within Italy that he exercised the authority that belonged properly to a metropolitan. If he exercised his patriarchal authority more broadly over the ecclesiastical provinces of the West, he also respected their legitimate autonomy and required that one take on the cultures proper to the evangelized nations.[58]

95. Undoubtedly, one must avoid idealizing the relationship among the patriarchal churches of antiquity, for at times they experienced serious difficulties. One might even question whether the "pentarchy" existed fully in reality, despite the conciliar statements cited above. Even so, the patriarchal structure enabled the achievement, at least to a certain extent, of a just relationship between the regional churches and the universal church and in this way encouraged good order in the exercise of doctrinal authority. Recalling this structure ought to allow regional and continental structures, with their legitimate particularities, to find their rightful place. Furthermore, it should enable us to differentiate the diverse functions of the see of Rome. Contrary to the quasi-coincidence of the patriarchate of the West and the Roman Catholic Church in the second millennium, the reference to the organizational structure of the early church ought to help us understand that that the pope does not administer that church by virtue of his responsibility in relation to the West. This responsibility must be distinguished from that which he exercises as bishop of Rome in service to the communion of churches scattered throughout the world.

58. See the letter of Gregory the Great to Mellitus on the evangelization of Great Britain (*Lettres.* XI, 76; *PL* 77, 1215-1217). In a letter to the Patriarch of Alexandria, he explicitly refused to accept the title "universal pope." "If your Holiness calls me universal pope, you deny to yourself that which you attribute in a universal sense to me. Let that not be so. Away with those words that which inflate vanity and wound charity." (*Lettres.* VIII, 30; *Pl* 77, 933 C); cited in J. M. R. Tillard, *The Bishop of Rome,* trans. John de Satgé (Washington, Del.: Michael Glazier, 1983), p. 52. Original version: *L'évêque de Rome* (Paris: Cerf, 1982.)

Section II: The Medieval Period

I. Prior to the Schism between East and West

96. During the High Middle Ages (from the eighth to the tenth centuries) there was a progressive erosion and then a fading out of the authority of the "pentarchy" as a form of collegial governance. As we have seen, pentarchy was a system whereby the supreme authority in the church was attributed to the five patriarchs of Rome, Constantinople, Alexandria, Antioch, and Jerusalem. This concept, promoted by Constantinople, or Byzantium, was received by the see of Rome with some reticence; it preferred the triarchy of the three sees founded by the apostle Peter: Rome, Alexandria, and Antioch. This system functioned in a somewhat formal manner from the second half of the fifth century. It did not survive the schism of 1054 except as a theoretical reference among the Orientals.

97. The pope exercised a different authority through his roles as metropolitan of the Province of Rome,[59] patriarch of the West, and minister of communion. The historical decline of the three patriarchates (Jerusalem, Alexandria, and Antioch) — above all, the anti-Chalcedonian reactions in these regions, the Arab conquests, and the political-religious tensions between Constantinople and Rome — contributed to the strengthening of Roman authority. Nicholas I refers to himself as the head of the "Apostolic See." A canon of the Roman council called to prepare for the ecumenical Council of Chalcedon IV declared:

> If anyone defies the dogmas, orders, prohibitions, sanctions, or decrees promulgated wisely by the head of the Apostolic See, whether pertaining to the Catholic faith, to ecclesiastical discipline, or to the reprimand of some faithful . . . let him be anathema.

In the East, the predominance of Constantinople as the see of the "Ecumenical Patriarch" also distorts the system of pentarchy.

98. Other authorities also played their part: local councils, theologians, and political figures. The relationship between the church and

---

59. The contemporary *Annuario Pontificio* still includes the title, "Primate of Italy, Metropolitan of the Province of Rome."

political leaders was a difficult one, as they constantly sought to exert their control over her. It is true that kings and other sovereigns, far from being "laymen" in the modern sense of the word, were considered sacred and viewed as ministers of the church. This was especially so in the case of the emperor, supreme chief of the "Christian people." We need only think of Charlemagne who considered himself the protector of the faith of his subjects against all heresy, condemned Spanish Adoptianism by introducing the *filioque* into the Credo, and developed his own version of the cult of images.

II. The Schism with the East and the Gregorian Reform (1049-1128)

99. The break with the East, which developed gradually well before 1054, and the pontificate of Gregory VII led in the West to a fixation on the unique authority of the pope.

100. By the end of the eleventh century, the papacy took the lead in a vigorous moral and institutional reform of the church. Through its legates, Rome became actively present in all regions of Western Europe. The lay nobility renounced a good many of their privileges, and the emperor was excommunicated and threatened with removal. In this context, the popes established themselves as the sole supreme legislators of Christianity. Gregory VII stands as the extreme example of this tendency. In his *Dictatus papae* (1075), the pope's authority is presented as the source of all powers in the church, or at least of their legitimization. Referring to the exercise of this authority in doctrinal matters, *Dictatus* 22 affirmed: "The Roman Church has never erred, and according to the testimony of Scripture, it will never err."

101. The conviction that the Roman see possessed the duty and the right to exert this authority over the whole church, as the source of all power, is again asserted in the twelfth and thirteenth centuries. Innocent III (1198-1216) calls himself not only the "Vicar of Peter," as did his predecessors, but "Vicar of Christ." Councils were not abolished. On the contrary, six were held in this period and considered by the Catholic tradition as "ecumenical": Lateran I (1123), II (1139), III (1179), IV (1215), Lyon I (1245), and II (1274). But these were held in the presence of the pope, according to a program which he established. They were more like a "recording studio" than a deliberative assembly. They dealt

primarily with matters of discipline, diplomacy, and political relations. However, these councils did treat a number of doctrinal questions, condemning the Cathar Gnostics, the neo-Donatist tendencies of certain anti-clerical sects, and, at Lyon II, taking a position on several points where East and West diverged.

102. During this period, the influence of scholastic theology expanded very rapidly. Its mode of thinking was deeply marked by a rational approach and widely imbued by canonical discipline. The "Masters" played a prestigious role in advising popes and councils. St. Thomas Aquinas would speak of a "magisterium of the Master's chair" *(magisterium cathedrae magistralis)* which he distinguished from the "magisterium of the Pastoral chair" *(magisterium cathedrae pastoralis).*[60] One spoke of the University as constituting a "third power" within Christianity, next to that of the pope and the empire. Yet, it was not a "counter-power" in competition with these others. It supported the hierarchy more than it contested or relativized its authority.

103. Certain "charismatic" personalities, such as Bernard of Clairvaux, also marked the life of the church in this period. Their views were listened to very closely, including by those who had the power of decision-making in doctrinal matters. For example, Bernard's influence was great in the condemnation of Gilbert de la Porrée's trinitarian theology by the councils of Reims and Lateran IV.

III. The Conciliarist Crises

104. The progression of Roman centralization during the Middle Ages did not follow a linear trajectory. The exile of the popes to Avignon, followed by the Great Schism of the West which saw the confrontation of two, and then three rival popes, would lead to a temporary eclipse of the papacy.

105. Conciliarism, which may be defined as an attempt to move the church from a model of absolute monarchy to one of constitutional monarchy, developed in several stages. The Council of Constance (1414-1418), which brought an end to the Great Schism of the West, declared that a council is superior to a pope under certain critical circum-

---

60. *Quodlibeta* III, 9 ad 3.

stances. The Council of Basel, which began under the authority of the pope in 1431 and was transferred by the pope to Ferrara in 1438 and then to Florence, continued in a state of schism with a decreasing number of prelates until 1449.[61] It established the formal terms of conciliarism, ruling that the pope owed obedience to the council and had no right to dissolve it, while the council could depose the pope if he chose to oppose it. This position was contradicted by the Council of Florence, which declared the supremacy of the pope over a council.

106. The councils of Constance and of Basel, which attended especially to questions of discipline and church governance, intervened in matters of doctrine, particularly of ecclesiology. The Council of Constance posthumously condemned the teaching of Wycliffe. His disciple Jan Hus, preacher and rector of the University of Prague, was burned at the stake, as was Jerome of Prague. Their "Bohemian revolt" protested against the practice of indulgences and for sharing the cup of the eucharist with the faithful.[62]

The conditions for the re-establishment of unity with Constantinople were also specified at this council. On these points, the partisans of both papal superiority and of the supremacy of the council were in agreement.

107. Over the course of the fifteenth century the role and the authority of theologians grew greater. In 1414, the Council of Constance included among its members doctors of theology and of canon law who were not bishops.

Summing Up the Lessons Drawn
from the Patristic and Medieval Periods

108. *The patristic period reflects the diversity of factors which contribute to the conferring of authority on an expression of doctrine. This authority depends, in part, on fidelity to the Scriptures and to the apostolic tradition. It could be linked to the quality of the persons intervening in the debates, or of the synodal and conciliar bodies which speak on a given question. It is also related to the very*

---

61. The assembly recognized by the pope established an ephemeral union of the Eastern and Western churches in 1435.

62. Luther would later say, "You can burn Jan Hus, but you cannot burn the truth."

way in which the gatherings of bishops or of churches operate, such as the effect produced in believers who are themselves called to "receive" the teaching of the bishops or councils. These factors often come together in diverse ways, yet they are all necessary for a correct exercise of doctrinal authority.

109. Somewhere between an essential fidelity to Scripture and the apostolic tradition (a principle strongly affirmed by Irenaeus) and the decisive requirement of ecclesial reception (something clearly evident in the history of the great ecumenical councils) is a place for different attempts to regulate and which aim to promote the path toward genuine unity. We see this, for example, when one appealed to the competence of Origen to resolve a doctrinal disagreement, when the bishops gathered take a position on a central question concerning the Christian mystery, when theologians like Cyril of Alexandria or John of Antioch manage to recognize their communion in faith beyond diverse theological language, or again, when Augustine strives to restore harmony between the African bishops and the bishops of Palestine. These attempts at regulation, which are sometimes the object of a theoretical elaboration (as in the case of Augustine or Vincent of Lerins), take place within a church gifted with regional structures which are at once autonomous and linked together. This organization is most notable in the form of the patriarchates, where the bishop of Rome himself exercises a patriarchal function in relation to the West, while at the same time in having a mission to preside over the communion of faith in relation to the universal church.

110. As we have seen, there were serious crises concerning questions of a properly doctrinal nature in the patristic period. Yet, if this period offers many lessons for the understanding of our subject, it is by the very way in which the church sought and invented forms of regulation which enabled it to surmount those crises and, in so doing, restore the bonds of ecclesial communion. Thus, we see that doctrinal authority is never acquired once and for all. Yet it is always possible by means of the churches' commitment to unity. This survey gives us some precious points of reference which ought to guide the churches and their leaders in the exercise of doctrinal authority when transposed into our present situation.

111. The Middle Ages were marked by the schism between East and West. Despite the many great moments witnessed in this period of Christian history, its negative consequences were incalculable. In the West, this break led to a certain distortion of earlier structures in favor of a centralization of authority in the hands of the pope. This centralization took place, for the most part, in the hope of reforming a church afflicted by abuse. However, the persistence of abuse even in the Roman court gave rise to the conciliarist crisis and the expression of protests which, as history has shown us, were forerunners of the sixteenth-century separation. Thus, the churches born of the Reformation held that the church of the late Middle Ages was not sufficiently faithful to the gospel. The Catholic Church, while recognizing the presence of abuses from the grassroots to the summit, always considered that the medieval church remained fundamentally faithful to its mission.

112. To sum up, this survey of our common past reveals that throughout history the church recognized the absolute authority of God, of Christ, and of Scripture over its life. We also see that the church was convinced of its own authority in teaching matters of doctrine — a paradoxical authority, which must be submissive to that which is greater than itself. We have attempted to gather examples of the exercise of doctrinal authority throughout history, with their rich diversity of modalities and developments, and to learn from how it was carried out in practice, according to its communal, collegial, and personal dimensions. This is our common heritage, with all its light and shadows.

113. We are not, however, advocating an anachronistic return to the forms of the past. Rather, this overview invites us to seek new ways of proceeding, grounded in tradition, and more flexible than those which have dominated in the course of the past two centuries. We shall return to this point in chapter four.

CHAPTER TWO

The Reformation and the Modern Periods

Section I: The Protestant Tradition and the Crisis of Authority

I. The Reformation and the Reformers

114. The Reformation's treatment of authority and power in the church is largely due to a critical and reforming reaction against a certain number of historical deviations, especially dating from the Middle Ages, which were strongly castigated by Protestantism. The understanding of the question of authority must be reconsidered in light of this twofold concern for critique and reform. The Reformation interpreted the problem from several perspectives: theological and doctrinal, ecclesiological and ministerial, ethical and disciplinary, juridical and political. We shall analyze the question primarily from this first perspective, that of *doctrinal* authority; that is to say, as it pertains to the formulation and communication of the content of faith.

115. Protestant Reformers contested the magisterial claims of the institutional church (popes and councils held after the patristic period) to be the only historical instance of interpretation, verification, and mediation of biblical revelation, that is, of the Scripture-Word bearer of the Truth. The Reformation based its opposition on the dissonance between the witness to the Truth given by the canonical Scriptures and the "truths" later formulated and imposed as normative for the faith.

116. To justify their fundamental questioning of authority the Reformers

appealed on the one hand to Scripture as the sole norm for doctrine *(norma normans)*, and, on the other, to the doctrinal statements which were later formulated by the church gathered in the great ecumenical councils (the confessions of faith understood as *norma normata*). In so doing, they contested the established church of their time (the medieval Roman church) in both its fidelity to the sources and its historical continuity.

117. How was it, in the view of the Reformers, that the medieval church could have so distorted the norms of authority? Their fundamental question referred above all to the matter of *interpretation:* if Scripture was to be read and interpreted according to a unanimously recognized canon, what authority could be ascribed to the authoritative interpretation of the magisterium beyond that of Scripture whenever it sought to explain, actualize, and even extend and communicate the content of the truth of Scripture?

1. Scripture Alone as Authoritative Reference

118. In faithfulness to the principle of justification by faith alone, and to the extent that Reformation theology considered every institution (including the church) as a human, and therefore sinful realization (a "work"), the first necessary and theologically sufficient magisterial principle *(norma normans)* for a faithful understanding and communication of the content of biblical revelation could only be the inspiration to which the Spirit gives rise in and through Scripture. "It is said, 'the Word of God — and no one else, not even an angel — should establish articles of faith,'" wrote Luther.[1]

119. The Reformers considered Scripture as bearing its own interpretive norm: "*Scriptura ipsius interpres,* Scripture interprets itself." In this perspective, the Word, the gospel, and Christ are synonymous, and Scripture carries the Word within itself just as it "carries Christ" (Luther). The Word, the gospel, and Christ are at once prior to and flow from Scripture. It has no need of any external authority to attest to its normativity. This position stood in opposition to the Roman Catholic theory on the establishment of the canon of Scripture, according to which the authority of the church was indispensable, and further, conferred this normativity. In this sense, the question of Scripture was a

---

1. Martin Luther, "Smalcald Articles (1537)," in *The Book of Concord: The Confessions of the Evangelical Lutheran Church,* ed. Robert Kolb and Timothy J. Wengert (Minneapolis: Fortress, 2000), p. 304.

christological question for the Reformers before it became an ecclesiological problem.

120. As the authority of the popes and of the established church's councils were considered to have broken with the unity of the faith, the Protestant Reformation henceforth substituted the rule of the *inner* testimony of the Holy Spirit, the only source of inspiration and interpretation capable of witnessing to and truthfully communicating the content of faith. Working in the individual and collective consciences of believers, the Spirit alone could bring about the understanding and interpretation of the biblical revelation. The Spirit was the only magisterial authority of the one tradition recognized by Protestantism, namely the unalterable "deposit of faith" consigned once and for all to Holy Scripture.

121. In defining the norm of authority in doctrinal matters, the Reformation took up a fundamental principle of Luther's theology, the distinction between the "inward" and the "outward." Anything arising from faith — grace, perfection, the newness of redemption, and the gift of the life of God in the human person — belongs to the *inner* domain. Whatever flows from the natural condition of the human person apart from God — sin, the law, imperfection, egocentrism, works, death — belongs to the *outward*. As it pertains to the domain of faith, the norm of authority arises from the *inward*. It is nonetheless mediated by the *outward*.[2] Thus, the biblical revelation in the form of Scripture belongs to the *outward* expression of faith, while insofar as it is Word (or gospel), it belongs to the *inward* reality. Fallible as human writing, it becomes infallible and normative when it is perceived in faith as the Word of Truth.

122. By linking the normative reference *(interior)* of the Word to the historical norm *(exterior)* of Scripture, the Reformation raised the question of the personal capacity for reading and interpretation *by faith* of each believer. The

2. Cf. *Wider die himmlischen Propheten, von den Bildern und Sakrament;* WA 18, p. 136. Here Luther reacts against the *illuminati* who confound the inward and spiritual, the outward and corporal, and believe that they can do without mediation of the Word through Scripture, sacraments, or other *outward* signs. "From the moment that God gave us the gospel, he gave it in two ways: as an outerward reality on one hand, and inner reality on the other. Insofar as it is an outerward reality, God addresses us in the word proffered in the gospel and through bodily signs such as baptism and the sacrament. As an inner reality, God speaks to us through the Holy Spirit, through faith and through the other gifts. Yet in all of this, he speaks to us in such a way that the outerward things necessarily precede the others. The inner realities follow upon the outward things, because God has not given to any man the inner things without the outward."

authority of interpretation must also move from the outward to the inward domain, from the institution to faith, from the letter to the Spirit, from imperfection to infallibility. However, when differences arise, or even conflicting readings and comprehension, who is to judge the veracity of the interpretation (by the individual or the community)?

123. By attributing the authoritative norm in these matters to the Holy Spirit, the Reformation leaves this question partially open. A permanent questioning of the Scripture as an interpreted text, confronted with the interpreting Word of Scripture, remained not only a possible risk but also an indispensable opportunity. Through this continual questioning the Reformation sought to maintain the sovereign freedom of the Spirit. The task of reading and of interpretation in the faith of believers was to be taken up anew in the course of history, in submission to the *viva vox Evangelii,* the living voice of the gospel. The expression attributed to the Reformers,[3] that the reformed church *(ecclesia reformata)* was always in need of reform *(semper reformanda)* would later underscore this continual questioning of the norm of authority that had always to be discovered anew.

2. Individual Liberty and the Collective Conscience

124. From an ecclesiological point of view — "outwardly" according to the terminology of the Reformation — there are two fields for the exercise of authority and Truth: (1) the *individual* person, the point of encounter of the human and of grace, the first and privileged place where Scripture becomes magisterium by the mediation of the Spirit; (2) the *communal* person of believers, the church, the second yet indispensable place where the Word must be spoken in truth, just as it has been received, interpreted, and expressed by the believer. Between these two points of reception and of understanding the truth of the gospel, *norma normans* and *norma normata,* a regulating and permanent dialectic must ensue to allay the recurrent tension between the individual believer and the community. This dialectic ought to overcome the permanent temptation to "muzzle the Spirit" (Martin Bucer) and to accord the status of normative, dogmatic, and suprahistorical truth to contin-

---

3. To our knowledge, the expression appears only in the seventeenth century.

gent interpretations, thus supplanting the *norma normans* by the *norma normata*.

125. The Reformation also considered the church as the communal context where the individual conscience of the believer developed and was lived out. In so doing it recognized that the church, in the ever unstable equilibrium of normative truth and historically conditioned statements, has a role to play in the formulation and the verification of the faith, its interpretation and witness, its "outward" and public expression. The Reformers sought to ward off the danger of rising individualism and of subjectivist inspiration, even though, in the end, it is always Scripture which, through the Holy Spirit, remains the ultimate judge, and not the church or the individual. "It is very unfortunate," warned Luther, "that everyone feels the need to enter into the Scripture with nothing but their head, to do with it whatever they please. Let no one think they are authorized to do so, unless they have been seized by the Holy Spirit."[4] Calvin criticized those "fanatics" who "abandoning Scripture and flying over to revelation, cast down all the principles of Godliness"; in so doing they "wrongly appeal to the Holy Spirit."[5]

126. Thus, the church can always rediscover the gift of the authentic ecclesial and public witness to the Truth[6] through an ongoing process of formation which moves from the individual to the communal. The Holy Spirit is the "teacher," the Scriptures the pedagogical setting, and biblical revelation the program. In the language of Protestant ecclesiology, the *primary* reference of interpretation and communication was transferred from the "visible" and institutional level ("outward") to the "invisible" and theological ("inward") level." Calvin wrote,

> But let us, on the other hand, avoid falling into the same pit, fix our ears, eyes, hearts, minds, and tongues completely upon God's sacred teaching. For that is the school of that best schoolmaster, the Holy Spirit, in which

---

4. Martin Luther, *Predigten über das 2. Buch Mose*, 1524-1527; WA 16, 68. 22-24.

5. John Calvin, *Institutes of the Christian Religion*, Library of Christian Classics XX-XXI, ed. John T. McNeill (Philadelphia: Westminster Press, 1960), I, IX, p. 93.

6. Consider the title of one of Luther's treatises: "That a Christian Assembly or Congregation has the Right and Power to Judge all Teaching and to Call, Appoint, and Dismiss Teachers, Established and Proven by Scripture (1523)," *Luther's Works*, vol. 39, trans. and ed. Eric W. and Ruth C. Gritsch (Philadelphia: Fortress, 1970), pp. 305-314.

we so advance that nothing need be acquired from elsewhere, but that we ought to be willing to be ignorant of what is not taught by it.[7]

3. Four References of Normative Authority

127. The confessions which codify the contents of faith, as they have been verified, recognized, and proclaimed, were not normative in the same way as Holy Scripture, which possesses the inner witness of the Holy Spirit. They played a role as a simple witness to a faith, not its master. Nonetheless, the *confession of faith [retained] a fundamental and vital function in the church.*[8] The exercise of authority was understood within a hermeneutical circle which maintains a balance and relationship between: (1) *Scripture* as the point of reference for the data of revelation; (2) *the individual conscience* as the first reference for the understanding of revelation; (3) *the communal* and public *witness* of believers as the ecclesial reference for the content of faith; and (4) the actualization of this witness in normative texts, understood as symbolic — *confessions of faith, ecclesiastical disciplines,* or *catechisms.* In the Reformation churches, authority and truth are defined according to these four normative points of reference, in the changing equilibrium of their diversity, unity, and complementariness.

128. For the Reformers, it would be impossible to identify a normative truth (the reflected image) with the instance of its proclamation (the reflective mirror). This fundamental distinction between public communication ("outward" expression) and an authentically inspired doctrine ("inner" reality) would conjure up the danger of an arbitrary division of the church.[9] While a personal understanding of the truth could never be "muzzled" by a truth that is communally recognized, the latter served nonetheless as a protection against the excessive interpretive autonomy of the individual believer. Doctrinal unity, according to Calvin, came at a cost. "These things are inseparable — that Christians are taught faithfully the Word of God, that they receive what is proposed [in the Scriptures] in their hearts and minds, that there be fraternal accord among them, speaking as with one voice and making a pure and simple confession."[10]

7. Calvin, *Institutes,* IV, XVII, p. 1413.
8. André Birmelé and M. Lienhard, *La foi des Églises luthériennes* (Geneva/Paris: Labor et Fides, 1991), p. 13.
9. Calvin, *Institutes,* IV, I, pp. 1018-1019.
10. John Calvin, "Sermon on the Epistle to the Ephesians," in *CO,* LI, p. 432.

129. By refusing to identify the normative truth of Scripture with the interpretive expression of the church, the Reformation brought about a reversal in the manner of conceiving authority from an ecclesial perspective. "Judging the doctrine" was no longer the sole privilege of upper ecclesiastical authorities (that is to say, the clergy) — the reference to "sole" is important here so as to avoid interpreting the words of the Reformers as being anti-authoritarian — but becomes the effective function of the whole community (the *laos*) of the baptized. The elaboration of the truths of faith belonged, of course, to the theologians and interpreters, but judging their conformity to the gospel was the responsibility of all believers. Luther writes:

> Human words and teaching instituted and decreed that only bishops, scholars, and councils should be allowed to judge doctrine. Whatever they decided should be regarded as correct and as articles of faith by the world, as is sufficiently proven by their daily boasting about the pope's spiritual law. One hears almost nothing from them but such boasting that they have the power and the right to judge what is Christian or what is heretical. The ordinary Christian is supposed to await their judgment and obey it. . . . Christ institutes the very opposite. He takes both the right and the power to judge teaching from the bishops, scholars, and councils and gives them to everyone and to all Christians equally. . . . [B]ishops, popes, scholars, and everyone else have the power to teach, but it is the sheep who are to judge whether they teach the voice [i.e., the words] of Christ or the voice of strangers [an allusion to John 10:4-8].[11]

4. Doctrinal Unity, Pledge of Ecclesial Unity

130. The doctrinal *unity* lived out by the different ecclesial institutions ought to verify and attest publicly (in Latin: *visibile*) to the normative character of the truths proclaimed. The universally recognized affirmations of the confession of faith (as the *norma normata*) give witness to the magisterial fidelity of the church dedicated to the gospel (as the *norma normans*). The unanimity of these statements demonstrated the essential respect that churches held for the Reformation principle of

11. Luther, "That a Christian Assembly or Congregation Has the Right and Power," p. 306.

justification by faith alone, considered as the safeguard against all human claims to magisterial authority *jure divino,* by divine right. For, writes Calvin, "God will show himself in the mirror of his doctrine, his image will shine forth," not that of humans.

131. The indispensable "mark" of ecclesial *unity* is recalled forcefully by the *Formula of Concord* of 1577. This fundamental "note" of the church was to verify the biblical authenticity of the truths proclaimed and be their stable, public witness:

> Fundamental, enduring unity in the church requires above all else a clear and binding summary and form in which a general summary of teaching is drawn together from God's Word, to which the churches that hold the true Christian religion confess their adherence. For this same purpose the ancient church always had its reliable creeds, which were not based upon private writings but on such books as were set forth, approved, and accepted in the name of the churches that confessed their adherence to a single teaching and religion.[12]

The conception of doctrinal authority that Protestantism sought to put into practice, required doctrinal unanimity as the expression of unity in the very midst of ecclesial diversity.

II. The Protestant Tradition after the Reformation

1. The Authority of the Individual Conscience

132. The Protestant Reformation would recognize, in the dual exercise of doctrinal authority — between Scripture and the teachings of faith — the basis of its rules for functioning. Already in 1577, when confronted with the controversies that began to divide Lutheran Protestantism, the *Formula of Concord,* in the "Solid Declaration," specifies thus the order that ought to exist between different forms of authority:

> Holy Scripture alone remains the only judge, rule, and guiding principle, according to which, as the only touchstone, all teaching should and must be recognized and judged, whether they are good or evil,

---

12. "Solid Declaration," in *The Book of Concord,* p. 526.

correct or incorrect. The other symbols, however, and other writings listed above are not judges, as is Holy Scripture, but they are only witnesses and explanations of the faith, which show how Holy Scripture has at various times been understood and interpreted in the church of God by those who lived at the time in regard to articles of faith under dispute and how teachings contrary to the Scripture were rejected and condemned.[13]

Scripture alone, by virtue of its inspiration, was magisterium, and not the post-canonical formulas, even though they may be a faithful expression of its content. In spite of the denials that history would inflict on this oft repeated affirmation, all the Protestant confessions of faith and "ecclesiastical constitutions" would repeat this principle, no matter what modalities they chose to put it into practice.

133. By diversifying and apportioning the normative referents of authority and truth among the four parameters outlined above (see no. 127), the Protestant tradition remained faithful to the theology of authority developed by the Reformers. Further, in the context of the post-Reformation period, it conferred a magisterial pre-eminence over any common instance of authority upon personal freedom, the foundation of the ecclesial reality of believers. Accentuating its opposition to the theology of the magisterium defined by the Catholic Church and the Council of Trent, Protestant ecclesiology carried out an apparently irreversible inversion concerning the role and the place of the ecclesial institution, by affirming that the personal relationship of the believer to Christ (vertical) always has priority over the relationship to the ecclesial community (horizontal). Thus, the latter could not claim in any way, through its human institutions or its doctrinal statements, to be the necessary and hallowed source of the saving truth in Christ.

134. By removing the rule of faith from the upper echelons of the church, in order to grant it first of all to the free consciences of believers through the Scripture and the inner witness of the Spirit, post-Reformation Protestantism ran the risk of upsetting the indispensable balance among the four parameters of authority that had been established by the Reformation. It left the necessary doctrinal unity of the Protestant churches in disarray. The peremptory affirmation of the freedom of conscience, field of the Holy Spirit's action, and henceforth invoked as the principle ecclesiological norm of the Reformers, provoked continual divisions within Protestantism as disagreements devel-

13. "Formula of Concord," in *The Book of* Concord, p. 487.

oped between theologians and ecclesiastical authorities. Doctrinal unity lost credibility and ceased to be the mark of the "Reformed catholicity" once claimed by the first Reformation churches.[14]

2. Authority: A Theological Task

135. Despite its unbalanced emphasis on the freedom of the individual conscience, the post-Reformation tradition left the communal and public role of codifying and regulating the expression of faith to the ecclesial institution, through its religious and civil authorities. A responsibility in the *theological* order for statements of faith was entrusted to a new authority, which would be given the task of composing doctrinal texts on one hand, and of verifying, ratifying, and validating these texts on the other. In each territorial church, newly created "academies" with their pastor-theologians were considered as the instance of authority best equipped to respect the absolute principle of the norm of Scripture. Pastors formed in these academies thus became agents for the interpretation, the affirmation, and the redaction of the truths of faith.

136. It was as much out of political necessity as by ecclesiological conviction that the Protestant tradition confirmed and emphasized the established authority of university authorities. It entrusted them with the magisterium of interpreting Sacred Scripture, so that the *faculties of theology* became the recognized guarantors of the *regula fidei,* the rule of faith for the community of believers. In the course of conflicts and divisions, the importance of the clergy (professors of the faculties and pastor-theologians) was progressively amplified. The clergy became an interpretative authority by which the Protestant tradition attempted to respond to the Roman magisterial authority on doctrinal and pastoral matters following the Council of Trent. The regime of confessional territoriality (the principle of *cuius regio eius religio,* "the subject takes the religion of the prince") consolidated the system of linking doctrinal authority to the theological schools.

14. See "The Second Helvetic Confession" of 1566, of the Swiss Reformed Churches: "A Simple Confession and Exposition of the Orthodox Faith": "one Shepherd of the whole flock, one Head of the body, and to conclude, one Spirit, one salvation, one faith . . . it follows necessarily that there is but one Church which we therefore call catholic." In *Creed of the Churches,* 3rd ed., ed. John H. Leith (Louisville: John Knox, 1982), article XVII, p. 141.

137. A monopoly by theologians and pastors for the interpretation of Scripture and the articulation of confessional texts was uncontested until the mid-nineteenth century when Protestant territories passed from the Ancien Régime to republican forms of governance. Tension between two instances of authority — faculties of theology and non-clerical ecclesial authorities — has been a source of both conflict and collaboration right up to our day (see the manifesto of one hundred and fifty German theologians opposed to the 1999 Lutheran-Roman Catholic "Joint Declaration on the Doctrine of Justification by Faith").

138. The other function of authority, that of a communal instance of verification, decision, and application, was assumed in an analogous manner in different Reformation traditions. In churches with a Reformed and presbyterial-synodal model, it fell to the "classes" or "companies of pastors," then to synods notably made up of ministers and a majority of lay persons. In churches of the Lutheran tradition, this exercise of authority fell to assemblies having a similar task, yet having a different structure; for example, to "consistories," superior consistories," "inspections," or other forms of authority closer to a personalized episcopate.[15]

139. The two-fold function of doctrinal and pastoral authority was exercised in this way through the centuries of confessional division, defined in the complementarity between individual reflection (a), its communal expression (b), in the critical exchange between the individual conscience (a') and instances of communal authority (b'). The four normative parameters of authority are applied in the majority of churches of the Protestant tradition according to these four empirical forms. The dialectic between the ongoing reinterpretation of Scripture and the continual redefinition of the confession of faith became characteristic of the identifying movement of the Protestant churches. Interior to the hierarchy of priorities at work between these two norms, the norm that *is authority* and the norm that *is authoritative* (the *norma normans* and the *norma normata*), a permanent interaction is established where Scripture confers its normative ecclesial authority on the confession of faith and where Scripture, in return, receives a continuously renewed confirmation of its authority from the confessing church, at once permanent and contingent, preceding historically

---

15. See Groupe des Dombes, "The Episcopal Ministry: Reflections and Proposals Concerning the Ministry of Vigilance and Unity in the Particular Church," *One In Christ* 14 (1978): 267-288.

and dogmatically pre-eminent. In this movement of unstable equilibrium, neither of the two instances can validly function without the other. Each one needs the other partner to find and exercise its authoritative role.

3. Authority Conferred to Political Power

140. To this one must add, from the sixteenth century onward, the new role that Reformation churches entrusted to *civil* authorities in doctrinal matters.[16] In the absence of a recognized *juridical* authority that could replace the system of Roman ecclesiastical law, which was henceforth contested in its role as a "catholic" authority able to validate "ecclesiastical ordinances" or texts of the confession of faith, the Reformation churches assigned the *jus reformandi* to temporal power (and not to the pastor-theologians) in the place of traditional episcopal authorities. A tension between magisterial and disciplinary authority, inherent in this marriage of the two powers, existed subsequently throughout the history of Protestantism in recurrent and often conflicting ways (consider, for example, the crisis of the Lutheran Church in Germany under the regime of Hitler).

141. Under the Ancien Régime, the elaboration of texts defining the truth of the faith (confessions of faith, ecclesiastical disciplines, catechisms, and liturgies) was entrusted to strictly clerical assemblies that gathered together teachers, pastors, and other recognized ministers. The decisions of these assemblies had to be ratified and publicly validated by the (constitutional) juridical power of the temporal authorities, princes, and local oligarchs. Under the republican regimes that emerged in the nineteenth century this juridical authority was assumed by synodal or consistorial assemblies. These were predominantly gatherings of the laity, and decisions were made by simple majority according to the parliamentary system imposed by the new temporal powers. In regions where the church maintained its bonds to the state, the civil authority remained the primary instance of juridical and social validation for the decisions taken by these ecclesiastical institutions (synodal or consistorial).

---

16. See Martin Luther, "To the Nobility of German Nation Concerning the Reform of the Christian Estates (1520)," in *Luther's Works,* vol. 44, ed. James Atkinson, trans. Charles M. Jacobs (Philadelphia: Fortress, 1966), pp. 123-217.

142. In spite of their number and diversity in the course of history, confessions of faith continually recall the four points of reference or "matrices" of the notion of doctrinal and pastoral authority: the Bible (and its reading) as primary norm; freedom of the individual conscience as the receiver of its reading; theologians and pastors as its interpreters; the confessions of faith as its actualization and public witness. These references of authority were called upon to function in a unifying manner in the following theological fields: the reading of scriptural texts; the personal confession of the believer; the understanding of the ministry of the church as a collegial priesthood of all the baptized (principle of "universal priesthood"); the theology of schools (universities) and the places for its elaboration; and the public proclamation of confessional texts unanimously recognized by the church (confessions of faith and catechisms). Together, these fields are governed by the evangelical and cardinal rule of justification by faith (alone), which (alone) can guarantee the absolute sovereignty of God over the church and the unity of faith among believers.

4. Doctrinal Unity within Institutional Diversity

143. In ecclesial practice and despite many internal divisions, the equilibrium among the four parameters of authority was to remain the guarantee *no matter what form of ecclesiastical governance* was in place. In all the confessional churches that sought to remain faithful to their reforming origins, the principle of the freedom of the individual conscience as a place of scriptural inspiration was always affirmed as a founding principle for legitimate diversity within the ecclesial body. Claims that would permit one to avoid the constraints of any ecclesial community in doctrinal matters, as if it might "muzzle the Spirit" on the pretext of doctrinal imperatives or the necessity of uniformity, would contravene the principle of justification by faith alone or that of the ministry of the church understood as a "universal priesthood" shared by all believers.

144. In view of this equilibrium between the four normative references of authority and of the dialectic between unity and diversity within the ecclesial body, the churches born of the Reformation could never assert the precedence *jure divino* of an authority or a truth tending toward uniformity which they would claim to possess in a permanent, magisterial, or vicarious manner. And though "minor" excommunication[17] was practiced by the consistories of certain Reformed Churches

---

17. That is to say, exclusion from the Lord's Supper.

under the Ancien Régime, it was implemented as a temporary disciplinary measure to safeguard *jure humano* against the threat to unity and not to exclude diversity of interpretation or in the practice of faith which was lived paradoxically as unanimous and plural.

145. The *synodal* or *consistorial assembly* — at different levels: national, regional, cantonal, and parochial — was the ecclesial institution in which the diverse norms of authority and unanimity would converge. In certain churches of the "Reformed" confession, this assembly functioned autonomously. In churches of the Lutheran or Calvinist traditions, these worked in collaboration with the temporal authorities invested with new ecclesial responsibility. The following emerged from such instances of ecclesial authority: the Augsburg Confession (1530), the Confession of La Rochelle (1559), the Second Helvetic Confession (1566), the Formula of Concord of the Lutheran Churches (1577), the Articles of the Synod of Dordrecht (1618), the confessions of faith produced by these churches during the seventeenth and eighteenth centuries,[18] or again, more recently, the Barmen Declaration (1938) and the Leuenberg Accord (1973).

146. In the territorial churches of the Reformation, synodal or consistorial assemblies thus took up the role once carried out by Roman Catholic *diocesan* structures. First in clerical form (until the nineteenth century), and later in a form where the majority was non-clerical (from the time of the republican régimes), these instances of authority functioned collegially and retained the three forms of decision-making power traditionally conferred on ecclesiastical institutions, namely: authority in *doctrinal* matters, in *disciplinary* (moral) matters, and in *juridical* (ordinances or constitutions) matters. However, this threefold authoritative power did not confer on the synods or consistories any legal means of obliging the faithful to abdicate the freedom of their individual conscience in favor of the demands (doctrinal, moral, or juridical) of public documents (confessions of faith or ecclesiastical constitutions).

5. A Contestable and Often Contested Authority

147. In the course of their history, Protestant churches attempted to remain faithful in theory to the reforming conception of authority, being careful to maintain the balance among the different parameters. However in practice, through different historical, social, and political con-

---

18. See *Confessions et catéchismes de foi réformée,* ed. O. Fatio et al. (Genève: Labor et Fides, 1986); *Confessions de foi réformées contemporaines,* ed. H. Mottu et al. (Genève: Labor et Fides, 2000).

texts, both the definition of the various references of authority and their application in the life of the churches became the object of recurrent criticism. At times, it proved impossible to realize the absolute preeminence and normativity of the scriptural principle; at times, the doctrinal normativity of the texts of the confession of faith was contested; at times, the legitimacy of freedom of conscience and its preeminence over all other criteria for belonging to the church was called into question. At other times, the binding power of the authoritative reference (*norma normata,* in this instance, the confession of faith) on the individual conscience was notably affirmed as having priority in polemical situations with antagonistic churches (for example, in France during the sixteenth and eighteenth centuries), as circumstances put the equilibrium of the four norms at risk. On the other hand, the priority given to the normativity of the confession of faith often served as a binding argument within other Protestant churches.

6. An Unstable Dynamic

148. As this historical analysis reveals, the problem of doctrinal authority in the Reformation churches is a recurrent crisis belonging to the very identity of Protestantism. This phenomenon has its origin in the principle of *ambivalence* dear to Reformation theology, in particular that of Luther. According to this theology, reality — of humanity, the world, and God — and the way it is perceived by humankind is always twofold, marked by complementary and contrary terms.

149. The principle of a paradoxical understanding of reality and of truth is found in the following domains: the *philosophical and theological* (for example: questions of the authority of truth, of faith and reason, of assertion and doubt, of mystery and revelation, of a merciful God and a God who judges . . .); *anthropological* (the "outward" and the "inward," the old and the new, the individual conscience and the communal confession . . .); *ethical* (sin and justice, merit and sanctification . . .); and *ecclesiological* (the visible and invisible church, the Word and Scripture, the Holy Spirit and the ecclesial magisterium . . .).

150. In Reformation theology, in particular that of Luther, who takes up and develops this new way of doing theology in the extreme, all terms close to the problematic of "authority and truth" are thought out and expressed in a dual

manner, in pairs. From this flows the fundamentally *dialectical* and *critical* character of Reformed and Protestant theological thought. To reduce this emphasis would be to neutralize its original and innovative aspect in the history of Western theology. The ever present Lutheran formula *simul-simul* illustrates this fact: the harmonious progression of thought from reason to faith which characterized medieval Aristotelian metaphysical theology was henceforth contested by the dialectic nervousness that characterizes the reforming manner of doing theology. In its investigative procedure for examining theological, ethical, and ecclesiological truths, all terms are simultaneously complementary *and* antagonistic.

151. Moreover, this ambivalence is considered as *total:* God is at once totally Love and Judge, humanity is at once totally just and sinful (see and compare the fundamental term of Luther: *totus — totally*). We can only know reality in and through this inevitable ambivalence. Any apprehension of the real that would fail to attend to this ambivalence, verified as much by human experience as by biblical revelation, belongs to "sophist" speculation (Luther) or an ideological fiction. According to Reformation thought, the human condition and human existence can only be perceived *in reality* and *truly* in the permanent experience of this paradox of the simultaneity and the totality of contraries.

7. From Ambivalence to Crisis

152. This principle of an ambivalent understanding of reality is applied by the Reformation to the conscience of the believer on one hand, and to the understanding of the church on the other. Attributed to the conscience of the believer as the normative locus of the truth, the principle of ambivalence would serve as a safeguard against any equivocal and uniform absolutization, any claims of infallibility, even of the conscience as norm of authority and truth. It was not the conscience that was raised to the level of a norm, but the Word of God — Christ — who makes himself heard there. Thus, the principle of individual conscience — or of inspiration — was itself constantly questioned in its normativity, in this case by the critical affirmation of the anteriority of the Word in Scripture and of its preeminence over any individual and private understanding.

153. Similarly, the principle of ambivalence served as an argument

against the excessive evaluation of any public, ecclesial, or temporal communal norm, and against its claim to be a preeminent norm of expression, verification, or codification of the truths of faith. The ecclesial statement of the confession of faith, by the same right as the individual conscience, certainly had to be reaffirmed in its normativity. Yet it was also contested in its potential claim of exclusivity. Inerrancy and infallibility, holiness and purity characterize well the normativity of authority and of truth such as they were understood and defined by the Reformation; at the same time, they are characterized by contingency and historical relativity, sinfulness and fallibility, infidelity and lack of faith.

154. Thus, apart from the contradictions, normative authority, and truth perceived in their fourfold dimension — Scripture, personal conscience, the confession of faith, and the church — were *absolute* authorities and truths, total, without sin, arising from God and not from humanity. In other words, christocentric authority and truth marked by the preeminence of Christ-Word and by his Spirit over any anthropocentric norm, whether it be the individual conscience or the ecclesial confession of faith. It is only under this quadruple, paradoxical expression and in this ever unresolved complexity that historical analysis can speak of the theological and practical dimensions of the problem of authority in Protestant ecclesiology.

155. By way of example, let us consider the theology and practice of the consecration (ordination) to ministry in present Reformed churches. The confession of faith of the consecrating church, formerly a text sworn by the new ministers as a verification of their true faith, has become a simple element of liturgical remembrance. If candidates are still examined on their principles for the interpretation of Scripture, they are no longer tested as to their dogmatic fidelity to the contents of that confession. This situation prevails in our day with varying degrees of radical practice from one Protestant church to the next.

156. Another illustration of this situation is the confirmation of baptism. As it was progressively introduced into the Reformation churches, following from the exhortations of Martin Bucer or of Luther's *Small Catechism*, successive generations of catechumens were interrogated and made a commitment by the formula dear to Luther. "Do you believe?" Today, this type of commitment on the basis of the confession of faith is progressively falling into disuse, with a few rare exceptions. The confessing witness of the catechumen is most often replaced or supplanted by a gesture of blessing by the church.

157. Yet another example is the contradictory debate agitating the Reformed churches of the Federation of Protestant Churches of Switzerland (Fédération des Églises Protestantes de la Suisse, FEPS). The whole problem of doctrinal authority exercised in a federative and synodal manner is exacerbated the moment the question of consecration (ordination) for ministry or the question of the practice of the sacraments arises.[19] Suffice it to mention the problem of the reception of the Faith and Order document *Baptism, Eucharist and Ministry* by these same churches, and the refusal of the majority of their delegates as a "general assembly" to acknowledge the consensual and referential value of this document in doctrinal matters.

Summary of the Lessons Drawn from the Reformation and from the Protestant Tradition

1. A Recurrent Questioning

158. A crisis of authority reappears in a Protestant church whenever a private and individual person or a communal and public instance disrupts the equality among the four parameters of authority[20] and claims an infallible supremacy, invoking for themselves — and not for God alone — an alleged inerrancy which is nonetheless shattered by the principle of ambivalence. Each new claim forgets that, in matters of faith, it can only come up against the constraint of consciences, contrary to the fundamental affirmation of justification by faith alone. The dialectic of the "two kingdoms," dear to Luther, implies that all human authority in matters of faith remains relative, rendering impossible any alleged infallible and definitively normative exercise.

159. This recurrent questioning, due to an ambivalent appreciation of all reality, is emblematic from the very beginning of the history of Protestantism. In a polemical manner and even before the "Protestant" movement gave rise to the new forms of church that would be called "Lutheran," "Reformed," and others, the sole authority in matters pertaining to the truth of faith remained the individual conscience and the absolute freedom demanded by the Reform movement in the 1520s and 1530s. Nevertheless, despite the new theological importance at-

19. See Fédération des Églises protestantes suisses — Conférence des Commissions de liturgie, *Convention au sujet des Ministères et de la Consécration et son commentaire* (Bern: FEPS, juillet 1999).

20. See above, no. 127.

tributed to the parameter of individuality, it was indeed the church, guarantor of the tradition and of scriptural truth, that was practically (organically and constitutionally) invested with doctrinal authority.

160. *Exacerbated continually by controversy generated by spiritualist tendencies, the crisis of biblical interpretation which caused repeated divisions among Protestant churches could only be surmounted by reaffirming the value of a certain institutional hierarchal ordering of the four norms of authority presented above. Within these churches the church's confession of faith was applied as a public and exclusionary parameter of normativity, whether it was under the authority of temporal powers (for example, through the principle of* cuius regio eius religio, *"the subject takes the religion of the prince") or under purely ecclesiastical authority. Whoever refused the ecclesial normativity of the confession of faith for reasons of their individual and private conscience was confronted and often exiled from the confessional territory. Thus the unstable equilibrium of the principle of authority and its fourfold normativity was in constant crisis.*

2. Challenges to the Hierarchy of Authorities

161. *There is another important issue that arises from this constant calling into question. Beginning from the era of the consolidation of Protestant "orthodoxies," in particular since the second half of the sixteenth century, the Reformation churches make the confession of faith into an institutional, visible, truthful, and obligatory reflection of the "deposit of faith" (tradition) on both the private and public levels. The distinction raised initially by the Reformers between "in public and in private —* publice et privatim" *(Bucer) was no longer respected. At the same time, these ecclesial communities sought to invest the so-called "true" church — the newly reformed church — with a function of magisterial authority called to regulate the fundamental data of the faith through the course of history. This explains the imbalance among the four norms of authority.*

162. *We note that these imbalances gave rise to a hierarchical ordering of the norms of authority in practical terms, though not theologically. This permitted the occasional and partial resorption of excesses of diversification which arose in alternating critical moments and more peaceful times. Nonetheless, the principle of the plurality of instances of authority continued to bestow on the problem a character of institutional dispute, with recurrent tensions and movements, often of a divisive nature.*

163. *This hierarchical ordering contradicts the initial reforming scheme and*

its theological vision. The inherent difficulty in the actual functioning of this system throughout history reveals the paradoxical risk of a disordered reduction, of contradiction between theory and practice, between the reforming event and its ecclesial institutionalization. The exercise of authority sank into an underhanded power struggle among the different instances where, in accord with the original reforming vision, none succeeded in asserting itself or justifying itself as the unique magisterial norm with priority over the others.

3. From Normativity to Exemplarity

164. In the course of five centuries of Protestantism, the problem of authority can be divided into two periods: the first from the sixteenth until the mid-nineteenth century; and the second from the age of Revolutions to our times. Both periods reveal the question at stake and the impossibility of reducing the results to a simple common denominator. The conception of an authority founded on doctrinal unity on the one hand, and its diversified application on the other, constantly give rise to contradictory results. This confirms the complex tension between the initial vision and its historical realization, between its fundamental theological affirmations and the successive ecclesiological compromises of an ecclesially divisive movement that was never integrated.

165. Until the mid-nineteenth century Protestant churches maintained the communal profession of a common doctrinal text as a principle of ecclesial authority, truth, and unity in matters of faith. Following the dispute of the Enlightenment and the rise of republican governments, these texts — for example: those of the early ecumenical councils, the Augsburg Confession (1530), the Later Helvetic Confession (1566), or any other text written and locally adapted through the centuries — if they were in effect maintained, became simple texts of exemplary reference. They are included in the ecclesiastical constitutions by way of confessional and political definition, but not as an obligatory norm in matters of authority or of the truth of faith.

166. The preeminent role of this instance of ecclesial authority thus receded in favor of a freedom of the individual member of the church making uncertain the normative and obligatory reference to community or to a common statement of faith. This is true for both ministers and for the faithful. Indeed, each Protestant believer can become his or her own magisterium in matters of faith. They are only accountable to their own inspired conscience, which now assumes the primary role in the hierarchy of the norms of authority. As a consequence there occurs, following the fall of the Ancien Régime, the rise of what may be called Protestant (ecclesial) individualism — considered beneficial according to some, unfortunate by others.

4. The Protestant Squaring of the Circle of Authority?

167. In its historical developments, the approach to the question of authority within the Protestant churches testifies to the importance of the principle of ambivalence dear to Reformation theology: ambivalence between the initial dogmatic scheme on one hand, and its historical and institutional practice on the other. These remain in constant dialectical tension and none of the instances of authority alone can claim a preeminence in fact. Whenever one of the four norms claims such preeminence in fact, this can only be in a contingent, disputable, and disputed manner. Historical circumstances will always bring about new instability by raising new questions. If the fact of a hierarchical ordering of the different references of authority enables us apparently to resolve the crisis, the pragmatic Protestant solution seems to confer on the question of doctrinal authority in the ecclesial institution a character of continual relativizing, ever uncertain and never satisfactorily resolved.

Section II: In the Catholic Church, the New Face of the "Living" Magisterium

168. Confronted by the challenge of the Reformation, the Catholic Church experienced an important development during the period from the modern era to the contemporary age which saw an entirely new face of the magisterium emerge. It is important for our study to analyze the main lines of this development, and to draw from this analysis the principal lessons to be learned.

I. The Council of Trent

169. The Council of Trent did not deal directly with the question of the magisterium, for there was too much opposition among the council fathers on this subject. The council was effectively led by papal legates, however, and the assembly did not contest their role. In practice, Trent represents a shift in the history of the Catholic Church's doctrinal

magisterium. Henceforth, the bishop of Rome would be recognized as having a role superior to that of all others when it came to the affirmation of doctrinal orthodoxy.

170. This brought an end to the era of conciliarism, of which Marsilius of Padua and William of Ockham had been the theorists in the first half of the fourteenth century, and which had, in its time, played a role in helping the church move beyond the imbroglio and scandal caused by the coexistence of several popes. Despite nourishing other currents of thought, this ecclesiology was unable to assert itself, particularly in France. The efforts of the popes to restore their authority, begun under Martin V (1417-1431), were finally crowned with success. At the same time, the distressing possibility of a heretical pope, once envisaged by medieval theologians and canonists, ceased to preoccupy the collective consciousness. It was henceforth accepted that the pope exercised authority over a council.

171. Several characteristics of the Council of Trent prove of particular interest for our research:

- Trent was a defensive council intent on adopting a stance in response to the Protestant Reformation. The council fathers drew up a very coherent body of doctrinal and pastoral documents. But given the tone of certain statements, as well as their partial and unilateral character due to the polemic against the Reformers, they signified the end of any hope for the restoration of unity within Western Christianity. On the other hand, this body of doctrine provided an effective instrument for carrying out a deeply desired pastoral and disciplinary reform.
- 172. The council was a work of university scholars, most of them religious. Indeed, Trent was distinguished by their presence in great numbers, especially from among the Dominicans and Franciscans. Their knowledge contributed to the development of the conciliar texts a precision that they would not have had otherwise. Yet this also gave the texts a rather abstract character, removed from the religious expectations of ordinary men and women in this period.

173. The Council of Trent maintained a large measure of flexibility in its presentation of what the church required of the faithful in the way of the adherence to the faith. It was not obsessed by a desire to mark out and monitor every expression of faith. For example, in mat-

ters of teaching, Trent judged that *the church could not err* in teaching this or that doctrine or by imposing such and such a disciplinary practice without necessarily condemning a different position.[21] The council appeals to a reduced sense of "infallibility" which is, more accurately, an "indefectibility." But it maintains a subtle interplay between that which the church deems it ought to require of the faithful in the name of its saving mission and that which it considers to be formally revealed or *irreformable*.

174. During the post-Tridentine period, the magisterium takes on, bit by bit, the "modern" form with which we are most familiar, including, in particular, a considerable strengthening of the magisterial authority of Rome and a hardening in both its formulations and condemnations. Throughout this period, its interventions were multiplied and their scope extended.

II. The Reception of the Council

175. The pace of the council's reception varied according to each country, often reflecting the state of its relationship with the papacy. Yet one can affirm that it had a real effect, because it responded to the deep yearnings for a catholic reform.

Indeed, the council furnished the churches that had remained attached to Rome with a coherent body of doctrine and pastoral directives which contributed to the rebuilding of unity. The agreement on papal primacy that it conveyed presupposed a prior preference for unity, an option chosen by the majority. Following the split of the Reformation, the question of unity became primary. For many (including Ignatius of Loyola and his companions), Rome was a new Jerusalem,

---

21. Concerning the indissolubility of marriage, for example, the council limited itself to affirming that "the church is not mistaken" when it teaches that the bond of marriage cannot be broken by the adultery of one of the spouses, and that even the innocent spouse could not contract another marriage so long as the partner lives. See canon 7 on marriage, "Trent, Session 24," in *Decrees of the Ecumenical Councils,* vol. II, ed. Norman P. Tanner (London: Sheed & Ward/Georgetown: Georgetown University Press, 1990), pp. 754-755. The council did not wish to condemn the practice of the Orthodox Churches in certain of these cases. All subsequent citations of conciliar texts taken are from this edition.

and it was symbolically placed over and above fragmentations into local churches. The entire work of the council was borne by the hope of reconstructing unity around Christ and his vicar on earth, the pope. In the eyes of contemporaries, unity held much greater importance than freedom, especially personal freedom. The service of unity justified the use of coercion when oral persuasion was no longer effective. This "mystical" conception of unity led many, who were otherwise conscious of human limitations and the possibility of authoritarian erring by the popes, to adopt a form of obedience that they attempted to apply even to their judgment.[22]

176. A contrario, the trauma of the breakup of unity never ceased to occupy the collective unconscious of the Catholic Church, and it especially influenced the magisterium's work. This important fact explains the hardening of doctrinal and juridical positions in the post-Tridentine period, in ways not known even in the medieval period:[23] the index, numerous excommunications, etc.

177. Further, this movement took place, beginning in the second half of the sixteenth century, against a background of social and economic crises, and of wars (often religious). These followed a dynamic and optimistic first half century, the "beautiful" sixteenth century, which took place during the rise of a hierarchical model of nation-states where the sovereign exercised a power that was increasingly centralized and strong, and thus, often came up against the claims of princes and kings to exercise of authority in religious matters.

178. The need to strengthen the unity of the portions of Christianity that remained attached to Rome and the desire to display the spiritual power of the papacy converged to accentuate the pope's magisterial authority. For, at a time when Rome was preparing to reform the manner of its operating on the world political and social scenes, it sought to compensate for its retreat by increasing its spiritual and doctrinal power.

179. The papacy was able to rely on the work of a rather large number of theologians, among whom Robert Bellarmine (1542-1621) held a particularly impor-

---

22. That is to say, an obedience that not only carries out orders, but that attempts to make the superior's point of view its own through the knowledge and will.

23. The medieval period saw a hardening of positions in other ways, for example, in the activities of the Inquisition.

tant place. Inspired by monarchies marching toward absolutism, he developed an ecclesiological model with the pope as supreme sovereign. The ascendancy of papal doctrinal authority did not take place, however, without resistance.

III. Resistance to the Intensification of Papal Authority

180. Successive popes would, more or less violently according to their personalities and the circumstances, encounter resistance from both national powers and local churches. The opposition was at once political and religious, as illustrated by Gallicanism in France. Related currents of thought were formed in most European nations.

181. Even though the term *Gallicanism* did not appear until the end of the nineteenth century, the idea to which it refers dates back to a much earlier time. The old medieval belief in a religious authority received by kings through the rite of anointing was still almost unanimously accepted. Most notably, the idea was supported at the time of the Council of Trent by a majority of jurists, by the faculty of theology of Paris, and by most bishops for whom the king was traditionally a protector against the encroachment of the mendicant orders backed by the pope. Francis I, for example, considered himself and was recognized as a priest-king, vicar of Christ, having received a mission to lead his people in unity and justice to the Kingdom of God. Similarly, Catherine de Medici felt it her duty to convene the Colloquy of Poissy (1561) in the name of the king, her son, to resolve the theological questions that divided Christians.

182. Building on conciliarist theories, the Gallicanism of churchmen reflected an ecclesiology based on their conception of a political power respectful of intermediary bodies. It was especially concerned to defend the pastoral and doctrinal autonomy of the bishops, together with that of the pope. Its representatives held that spiritual authority was given by God simultaneously to the pope and the bishops, but in such a manner that the doctrinal and disciplinary decisions of the pope had no authority in themselves *(ex sese)* but only with the consent of the church *(ex consensus ecclesiae)*.

183. In this current of thought we encounter the great figure of Bossuet, defending the indefectibility of the church. If it committed errors, he held, these could not take root in the faith of the Church of Rome, but could only be associated with the person of the current

pope. The following proposition, written by Bossuet and promulgated by the Assembly of the Clergy of 1682, was condemned in 1794: *"In questions of faith the sovereign pontiff plays the primary role, and his decrees concern each and every one of the churches. His judgment is nonetheless not irreformable, unless it is supported by the consent of the church."*[24] The rejection of this line of thinking inspired the final redaction of the definition of papal infallibility at Vatican I.

184. The drive toward the centralization of doctrinal authority was also influenced by Jansenism, a movement in France that showed tendencies similar to those of Gallicanism. Antoine Arnauld first spoke publicly in 1656 of the legitimacy of a "respectful silence" required by deference due to the Roman pontiff before teachings that one judges to be false. This was his attitude with regard to the Constitution *Ad sanctam* of Alexander VII which condemned five propositions considered as belonging formally to the *Augustinus* of Jansenius. Arnauld distinguished between law and fact: by law the positions were condemnable, but in fact they were not to be found in the work of Jansenius.

185. The question flared up again in the early eighteenth century. Clement XI formally condemned the "respectful silence." Fenelon, a determined opponent against Jansenism, intervened. He considered the church to be infallible not only in matters of dogma, properly speaking, but also in non-revealed dogmatic facts, as was, for example, the case regarding the condemned propositions that were to be found in the work of Jansenius.[25] Fenelon's point of view stirred up the opposition of numerous theologians. In contrast, those in Roman circles encouraged him to defend the personal infallibility of the pope, something he refused to do.[26]

186. The desire for centralization thus provoked debates and encountered opposition. However, none of these proved to be insurmountable. The drive toward centralization was achieved, however, at great cost. Little by little, especially during the course of the eighteenth century, we witness the diminution of various ways of expressing the

---

24. Cited by Bernard Sesboüé, *Histoire des dogmes,* t. IV: *La parole du salut* (Paris: Desclée, 1996), p. 183.

25. It is not certain that Fénelon gave the term *infallibility* its present meaning, which includes the irreformability of an affirmation. On this question, see J.-F. Chiron, *L'infaillibilité et son objet. L'autorité du magistère infaillible s'étend-elle aux vérités non-révélées?* (Paris: Cerf, 1999), pp. 71-119.

26. L. Cognet, "Fénelon," *DGHE* (1967) t. XVI, col. 983.

faith experience of believers, to the advantage of the magisterium. This meant the end of the magisterium of the theologians, of whom nothing more would be required than a theological justification for papal positions. It was also the end of the authority exercised by mystics and of the freer expression of spiritual experience that their teachings had offered since the Middle Ages.

187. So much rigorism and often the defiance of local authorities ended up tarnishing the image of papal authority. During the course of the eighteenth century, there was a slow erosion in diverse forms of seeking religious consensus and a slow drift away from traditional forms of religious life. The argument from authority becomes less appealing.

IV. From Trent to Vatican I

188. No council was held by the Catholic Church after Trent (1545-1563) until Vatican I (1870). Within the historical context described above, this fact is the sign of a change in the shape of the exercise of the magisterium and of a certain number of shifts, all of them related, that one might characterize very schematically as follows:[27]

189. A shift from the *tradition* handed on toward the *instrument* responsible for handing it on and expressing it, the system that one would henceforth call the "living magisterium." At the same time, the question of proof shifts from the *source* of truth to the *authority* which guarantees that truth. The criteria of truth is located above all in that authority.

190. A shift from *fides qua*, that is to say from faith as a movement of adhesion, to *fides quae*, meaning faith as right knowledge. Thus, the magisterium becomes the direct conduit for this knowledge and the motive for the assent of faith understood above all as obedience to the church.

191. A shift from the *testimony* to the faith by the doctrinal authority of the church to the *determination* or definition of faith by that authority. It is from this context that the term *magisterium* emerges in the sense that we give it today.

192. A shift from the *indefectibility* (or inerrancy) of the church to the *infallibility* of the magisterium of the church. The charism of infallibility which belongs to the whole church is concentrated in the holders of magisterial authority. This infallibility is progressively connected with the idea of *irreformbility*. We

27. See J.-F. Chiron, "Le magistère dans l'histoire," *Recherches de Sciences Religieuses* 87 (1999): 483-518.

also witness the appearance of the term *definitive* which can be understood either according to its juridically accepted meaning (applied to a decision against which there is no possible recourse), or according to its doctrinally accepted meaning, where it becomes more or less a synonym for infallible.

193. A shift from the expression *fides et mores* in the broad sense, still in use at the Council of Trent, and aimed at the discipline of Christian life, to a narrower meaning of the term to designate the revealed truths concerning faith and moral doctrine.

194. A shift from the indefectibility of the dispersed church (the universal episcopate) to the infallibility of the Roman pontiff (and of a council). This constitutes a double movement toward a more restrictive meaning: from indefectibility (a broad concept) to infallibility (a narrow concept), and from the universal church to a council or, above all, to the Roman pontiff.

195. A development in the concept of the assent due to the decisions of the magisterium which raises the question of the nature and level of assent required, of "respectful silence" and of "dissent."

V. The First Vatican Council

196. The First Vatican Council and its definitions can only be properly understood within the perspective of the history of the church and of the papacy in the nineteenth century, including the historical, political, cultural, ecclesial, and theological factors that contributed to the rise in the power of the papacy.

197. The definitions of Vatican I are in fact bound up with the Catholic Church's perception of its historical situation at the time. It defined and expressed itself in opposition to the trend of militant and ideological secularization in civil societies (the ideas of 1789, the principle of nationalism, democracy, and, soon after, class struggle). Assuming a defensive attitude, it positioned itself as a parallel counter-society. Papal infallibility ought to be understood "as a pathetic protest for permanence at a moment when the material foundation of its power was crumbling."[28] In this period the Catholic Church experienced a triple trauma: *ecclesial* (in reaction against conciliarism and

---

28. C. Langlois, "L'infaillibilité, une idée neuve au XIXe siècle," in *Église infaillible ou intemporelle? Recherches et débats* (Paris: Desclée de Brouwer, 1973), p. 76. This paragraph is largely inspired by the discussion found here.

Gallicanism), *political* (in reaction to the system of national churches), and *intellectual* (in reaction against liberalism and secularism).[29]

198. The definitions of Vatican I are in keeping with an ecclesiology that developed "under the sign of the affirmation of authority" (Yves Congar).[30] This ecclesiology borrowed its categories from political philosophy.[31] The concept of *sovereignty* refers to a supreme power that is not bound by any external consent.[32] This model of absolute monarchy is applied to the pope's primacy of jurisdiction (that is to say, the governance and discipline of the church). Certain fathers at Vatican I wanted to extend this sovereignty of the pope to matters of *doctrine*. The definition of infallibility was thus required as a necessary complement to the primacy of jurisdiction.

199. Three identifiable groups were present at Vatican I: the extreme infallibilists, few in number, yet close to Pius IX; the minority (20 percent), reticent or opposed to the extreme concept of infallibility; and the "majority," favorable to infallibility, yet sensitive to the concerns of the minority and seeking a middle ground. The fundamental issue at stake was to know how the pope, when exercising his magisterium, would rely on the witness of the church's tradition. Could one take it for granted that the pope would always express the faith of the church? Or would the pope be required to seek assurance from the bishops concerning the faith of the church before making a pronouncement? Should such a consultation be an obligation and a *sine qua non* condition?

29. See, on this point, Hermann J. Pottmeyer, *Towards a Papacy in Communion: Perspectives from Vatican I and II,* trans. Matthew J. O'Connell (New York: Crossroad, 1998), ch. 3, pp. 36f.

30. We encountered this ecclesiology in our earlier study, *Le ministère de communion dans l'Église universelle* (Paris: Centurion, 1986), where we spoke of the definition of papal primacy at Vatican I. What we stated there applies equally to the definition of infallibility: "The First Vatican Council can appear as the triumph of the personal ministry of unity in the church. The Bishop of Rome is henceforth venerated as head and infallible sovereign pontiff by all Catholics who see in him the irrefutable sign of their Christian identity. This, in spite of the terms chosen deliberately to limit his 'charism of truth.' He can represent, he alone, the whole church" (no. 82). The two definitions of Vatican I are closely linked: the infallible magisterium of the pope appears as a necessary element of the full exercise of the primacy of jurisdiction.

31. See the emblematic work of Mauro Cappellari — the future Pope Gregory XVI — published in 1799, *Le triomphe du Saint-Siège et de l'Église contre les assauts novateurs, combattus et réfutés avec leurs propres armes.*

32. The celebrated formula of Pius IX, "La tradition, c'est moi," is a reply to that attributed to Louis XIV, "L'état, c'est moi."

200. In the "Dogmatic Constitution on the Catholic Faith," *Dei Filius*, approved before the document on infallibility, we find the establishment of several concepts concerning the subject of the magisterium that would become classic:

> Wherefore, by divine and catholic faith all those things are to be believed which are contained in the word of God as found in Scripture and tradition, and which are proposed by the church as matters to be believed as divinely revealed, whether by her solemn judgment or in her ordinary universal magisterium.[33]

The text indicates two modes for the exercise of the magisterium: an act of solemn judgment, or the "extraordinary magisterium," that is to say, definitions promulgated by councils (or eventually by the pope, as was already under discussion); or second, the "ordinary universal magisterium," that is, the current teaching of the pope and the bishops on a point that is taken as self-evident (for example, the divinity of Christ prior to its definition by the Council of Nicaea). The two adjectives "ordinary and universal" are related. There is no such thing as an ordinary magisterium that belongs to the pope alone.

201. The definition of papal infallibility is formulated in the following manner:

> . . . when the Roman pontiff speaks *ex cathedra*, that is, when, in the exercise of his office as shepherd and teacher of all Christians, in virtue of his supreme apostolic authority, he defines a doctrine concerning faith or morals to be held by the whole church, he possesses, by the divine assistance promised to him in blessed Peter, that infallibility which the Redeemer willed his church to enjoy in defining doctrine concerning faith or morals. Therefore, such definitions of the Roman pontiff are of themselves, and not by the consent of the church, irreformable.[34]

---

33. First Vatican Council, "Constitution on the Catholic Faith, *Dei filius,*" in *Decrees of the Ecumenical Councils,* vol. II, ch. 3, p. 807.

34. First Vatican Council, "First Dogmatic Constitution on the Church of Christ, *Pastor aeternus,*" in *Decrees of the Ecumenical Councils,* vol. II, ch. 4, p. 816. The council used the term *held* and not *believed,* intending to leave open the question of whether infallibility extends to points that are connected to revelation. The interruption of the council meant that it was not possible to treat this matter in the *Dogmatic Constitution on the*

202. To interpret this text accurately, we can turn to the important report of Bishop Gasser, president of the council's doctrinal commission, which presented the text to the council fathers prior to their voting. This report reflects the official position of the commission that wrote the text.[35] The reporter shows that Vatican I did not adopt the position of the extreme infallibilists and that recurrent maximalist interpretations of infallibility do not correspond to the intention of the authors.

203. Did the text define an *absolute, personal,* and *separate* infallibility?

Absolute? Gasser responds that "absolute infallibility belongs only to God alone," and that papal infallibility is limited in three ways: first, *as to its subject,* when the pope acts as a universal teacher and in relation to the universal church. He does not enjoy this charism as a private person or as a private teacher. Next, it is limited *as to its object:* it pertains to that which belongs to the apostolic tradition and to the common faith of the church. Finally, it is limited *as to its enactment:* it concerns cases where the pope speaks *ex cathedra* by virtue of his apostolic authority.

Each time papal infallibility is circumscribed by an *only.* In this spirit, the two codes of canon law from 1917 and 1983 state, "No doctrine is understood as defined infallibly unless this is manifestly evident" (CIC [1917] 1323, 3; CIC [1983] 749, 3).

204. A *personal* infallibility? No, because this charism is not given to the pope as a private person, nor as a habitual quality. His inerrancy is limited to acts which can be determined in a precise manner.

205. A *separate* infallibility? This was the most debated question pertaining to the definition of infallibility at Vatican I. For the minority, it was vitally important that the pope not be separated from the church and that he not act separately. However, the final definition sounds a note of concern regarding this subject: "such definitions of the Roman pontiff are of themselves, and not by the consent of the church, irreformable."

Gasser specifies the meaning of these concepts[36] in speaking of a *distinct,*

Church. The question of the "secondary object" of infallibility would come up again after Vatican II.

35. Gasser's report is cited by the Second Vatican Council's "Dogmatic Constitution on the Church, *Lumen Gentium,*" in *Decrees of the Ecumenical Councils,* vol. II, no. 25, notes 43-46, p. 870. [All subsequent citations from the documents of Vatican I and II in the body of the text are taken from this edition. — Trans.]

36. Yet when he spoke, the precise formula "of themselves, and not by the consent of the church *(non ex consensu ecclesiae)*" had not yet been added to the definition; at the time, it contained only the words "of themselves."

yet not *separate* infallibility. The pope is only infallible in his role as "representative of the universal church." "We do not separate," the reporter states further, "the pope defining infallibly from the cooperation and collaboration of the bishops, at least in the sense that we do not exclude their cooperation and collaboration." The bond between the pope and the church is obvious, since a definition is only justified in the case of a grave disagreement in matters of faith and the pope only intervenes when disputes cannot be resolved at the regional level by the bishops. On the other hand, "the pope, by virtue of his responsibility, and according to the gravity of the situation, is bound to make use of the means best suited to examine the truth, just as he is to state it clearly. These means include councils, as well as the advice of bishops, cardinals, theologians, etc." But the necessity of this principle is not expressed in the definition in the form of an obligation. According to the reporter, doing so would call the whole thing into question and would lead to a "divided primacy."

206. The same is true with regard to the consent of the church: "We do not separate," says the reporter, "not at all — the pope from the consent of the church, on the condition that this consent is not stipulated as a condition. We cannot separate the pope from the consent of the church because this consent is never lacking."[37] According to Luke 22:32, Jesus said to Peter, "I have prayed for you that your own faith may not fail." It is to Peter that falls the task of confirming his brothers, not the other way around.

In short, Gasser affirms the minority in its concern to maintain a relationship between the pope and the consent of the church, yet he did not want this bond to take the form of a juridical obligation.

VI. From Vatican I to Vatican II

207. The dogma of papal infallibility would be interpreted in three different ways:

The *maximalist interpretation* which corresponds to the position of the extreme infallibilists. The central idea — rejected in Gasser's report — was that the infallible authority of the pope is the source of the infallibility of the church. It tends to eliminate the distinction between an *ex cathedra* definition and the other doctrinal declarations of the pope. It favors a centralization of doctrine. Even though this interpretation was not supported by many theolo-

---

37. In fact, the final formula of the definition is directed at the fourth article of the Assembly of the Clergy of France, 1682, mentioned above. This article claimed the need for a formal and subsequent agreement by the bishops that would *confer* the irreformable character of a decision.

gians, this simple approach made great inroads in the popular opinion of many Catholics.

208. The *middle-ground interpretation* held strictly to the letter of the council's teaching and contested the widespread misunderstanding of papal infallibility. This was the most widespread interpretation prior to Vatican II. However this interpretation, also unilateral in its approach, could give rise to the idea that those things about which the council did not speak explicitly — such as the collegial structure of the bishops' magisterium, the sense of the faithful, or reception — were nonexistent or without any doctrinal importance. Thus, "the danger of the middle-ground interpretation of the infallibility dogma is that it encourages the same tendency and practice as does the maximalist interpretation. . . . However, it is distinguished from the maximalist interpretation by the fact that it, like the definition itself, remains [at least theoretically] open to a reformulation of papal infallibility in the context of an ecclesiology of communion."[38]

209. The *third interpretation* corresponds to the concerns of the minority at Vatican I. It referred to the tradition of the first millennium, which understood the church as a communion of churches, and saw the pope exercising his magisterium (and his primacy) as head of the college of bishops, in concert with those who, like himself, shared in a responsibility for the universal church. Infallibility, which is promised first to the church as a whole, was only conferred on the magisterium of the pope and the college of bishops in relation to the whole church. The pope was not to put it into practice except in a subsidiary fashion, in case of urgent necessity and as a last resort, in cooperation with the bishops.

210. We note that the only occasion where the pope has exercised his infallible magisterium since 1870 was in the definition of the Assumption of the Virgin Mary by Pius XII in 1950. This definition was preceded by a formal consultation of the entire episcopate. Yet the definition was not made necessary because of any crisis where the faith was in peril, though this was the type of situation envisioned to justify the definition of Vatican I.

211. Since the nineteenth century, the Roman magisterium has multiplied its interventions and taking of positions, especially through the means of *encyclicals* that are recognized as having a great deal of doctrinal authority. This context raises the question of whether the everyday magisterium of the pope can be qualified as "ordinary," poten-

38. Hermann J. Pottmeyer, *Towards a Papacy in Communion*, p. 106.

tially infallible, as is the ordinary and universal magisterium as a whole. The concept of a diffuse infallibility has spread far beyond that which was taught by Vatican I.

VII. The Second Vatican Council

212. Vatican II took up the question of the magisterium once again and treated it as a whole. The Constitution on Divine Revelation, *Dei Verbum,* defined the relationship between Scripture and tradition on one hand, and the responsibility of the magisterium on the other:

> The task of authentically interpreting the word of God, whether in its written form or in that of tradition, has been entrusted to those charged with the church's ongoing teaching function, whose authority is exercised in the name of Jesus Christ. This teaching function is not above the word of God but stands at its service, teaching nothing but what is handed down, according as it devotedly listens, reverently preserves and faithfully transmits the word of God, by divine command and with the help of the Holy Spirit. All that it proposes for belief, as being divinely revealed, is drawn from the one deposit of faith. (*DV* 10)

The emphasis is on the subordination of the magisterium to the Word of God, and on the fact that it functions in the service of that Word which is its norm.

213. *Lumen Gentium* affirms first of all that the whole people of God is the subject of the infallibility of the church:

> The universal body of the faithful who have received the anointing of the holy one (see 1 John 2:20 and 27), cannot be mistaken in belief. It displays this particular quality through a supernatural sense of the faith in the whole people when "from the bishops to the last of the faithful laity," it expresses the consent of all in matters of faith and morals. (*LG* 12)

The *sensus fidelium,* the *sensus fidei,* is borne by all the baptized in an infallible way. From this, it becomes immediately clear that, if certain ministries in the church have a proper responsibility with regard to the proclamation and the regulation of the faith, these ministries are situated *within* the people of God and cannot be exercised except in communion with it.

214. The teaching function is presented as constitutive of the episcopal office, as are the offices of sanctifying and governing. The teaching office is no longer linked to jurisdiction as it was in the old schema of episcopal functions that included only two terms (order and jurisdiction). This office is exercised in communion with the head and the members of the college (see *LG* 21).

215. Preaching is the principal task of the bishops, who are called *authentic* teachers, a new term signifying the fact that they are vested with the authority of Christ to preach the faith. They are to be respected as "witnesses to the divine and catholic truth." The faithful are to adhere to their judgment in matters of faith and morals "with a religious assent of the mind." Finally, "the religious assent of will and intellect is to be given in a special way to the authentic teaching authority of the Roman pontiff even when he is not speaking *ex cathedra*" (*LG* 25).

216. The same term, *authentic*, is used to qualify the "everyday" teaching of the pope and the bishops. The "religious assent of will and intellect" designates an attitude which is not a formal act of faith.

With regard to the everyday teaching of the pope, it is specified that the authority of the documents he promulgates must be discerned according to the usual rules of interpretation (the nature of the documents, their intention, the manner of expression, etc.).

217. The first affirmation concerning infallibility concerns the college of bishops united with the pope:

> Although individual bishops do not enjoy the prerogative of infallibility, nevertheless, even though dispersed throughout the world, but maintaining the bond of communion among themselves and with the successor of Peter, when in teaching authentically matters concerning faith and morals they agree about a judgment as one that has to be definitively held, they infallibly proclaim the teaching of Christ. (*LG* 25)

This text is referring to what Vatican I called the "ordinary universal magisterium." But where Vatican I had said "proposed by the church in matters to be believed as divinely revealed" Vatican II says,

"they agree about a judgment as one that has to be definitively held."
This second formula, the interpretation of which is a sensitive matter,
seems to be more widely applicable. If it is no longer the adherence of
faith properly speaking that is required, that which is proposed (infallibly) as having to be "definitively held" can extend beyond what is properly revealed.[39]

218. The document then mentions the extraordinary magisterium
of the bishops gathered together in council:

> This takes place even more clearly when they are gathered together
> in an ecumenical council and are the teachers and judges of faith
> and morals for the whole church. Their definitions must be adhered
> to with the obedience of faith. (*LG* 25)

219. The following development concerns the infallibility of the papal magisterium. As with the infallibility of the church, papal infallibility "extends just as far as the deposit of divine revelation that is to be
guarded as sacred and faithfully expounded" (*LG* 25). Thus, the deposit
of revelation constitutes both the limit and the criteria for the extent
of infallibility.

220. The declaration of infallibility by Vatican I is taken up with
several variants in the teaching of Vatican II (indicated in italics):

> The Roman pontiff, *head of the college of bishops*, by virtue of his office,
> enjoys this infallibility when, as supreme shepherd and teacher of all
> Christ's faithful, *who confirms his brethren in the faith (see Luke 22:32)*, he
> proclaims in a definitive act a doctrine on faith or morals. Therefore
> his definitions *are rightly said to be* irreformable of themselves, and
> not from the consent of the church, *for they are delivered with the assis-
> tance of the Holy Spirit which was promised to him in blessed Peter; and
> therefore they have no need of approval from others nor do they admit any
> appeal to any other judgment.* (*LG* 25)

The additional qualifications integrate certain explanations from
Gasser's report given at Vatican I. We note especially the interpretation
of the final formula of Vatican I: the "not from the consent of the

---

39. Yet all that is proposed unanimously by the bishops is not necessarily infallible.
The teaching in question must also be proposed as needing to be "definitively held."

church" has a juridical value. A papal definition does not need to be approved by another instance, and it is not possible to appeal his judgment.

VIII. Since Vatican II

221. After a time of relative calm in the years immediately following Vatican II, the role of the Roman magisterium increased considerably, without a comparable growth in the collegial exercise of the bishops' magisterium. The synod of bishops no longer publishes its own documents, and the magisterial function of the episcopal conferences is strictly supervised.[40]

222. The publication of the encyclical letter *Humanae Vitae* in 1968, forbidding the use of artificial contraception, was an important event with regard to our study because of the controversy surrounding it. These debates contributed most notably to a rediscovery of the notion of "reception." If the theme of the *sensus fidei* was present at Vatican II, its link to the reality of reception was not mentioned in the conciliar documents. The first studies relating to this question date from the 1970s.

223. The 1973 declaration *Mysterium Ecclesiae* reaffirmed the classical doctrine of infallibility.[41] Yet it also contained an important new development concerning the *historical character of doctrinal statements,* including the formulation of dogmas.

224. Serious questions have been raised by a certain number of recent documents, including the 1989 profession of faith,[42] the Instruc-

40. See John Paul II, "The Theological and Juridical Nature of Episcopal Conferences," *Origins* 28 (July 30, 1998): 152-158.

41. Congregation for the Doctrine of the Faith, "In Defense of Catholic Doctrine," *Origins* 3 (July 19, 1973): 97, 99-112. This document was aimed especially at the position held by Hans Küng in his book, *Infallibility? An Inquiry,* trans. Edward Quinn (Garden City, N.Y.: Doubleday, 1971). Original version: *Unfehlbar? eine Anfrage* (Zürich: Benzinger, 1970).

42. Congregation for the Doctrine of the Faith, "Formula to Be Used for the Profession of Faith and the Oath of Fidelity [*Professio Fidei*]," *Origins* 18 (March 16, 1989): 661, 663.

tion *Donum veritatis* (1990),[43] and the motu proprio *Ad tuendam fidem* (1998).[44] We shall consider two of these texts.

225. The first question concerns the domain of truths subject to the teaching of the church. Where one had traditionally distinguished two "categories," the profession of faith and the 1990 Instruction introduced a new "category" of truths. The first traditional category referred to those truths belonging to revelation, which were taught as such by the church, and pertain to the realm of faith. The third (or second traditional) category relates to the everyday authentic teaching of the pope and the bishops to which the faithful respond by "religious assent of intellect and will." The new category is inserted between the two previously mentioned. It refers to "truths which are definitively taught by the church," which do not belong to revelation, but which are considered as "necessarily connected with divine revelation."[45] The assent required is "founded on faith in the assistance of the Holy Spirit to the magisterium and on the catholic doctrine of the infallibility of the magisterium." This category raises certain difficulties that have yet to be clarified.

226. The second question is raised by putting forward a new form for the exercise of the papal magisterium. The pope may, without formally engaging his infallible teaching office, declare by an act of his authentic magisterium that a doctrine pertaining to faith or morals belongs to the infallible teaching of the "ordinary universal magisterium of the bishops in communion with the pope." If this were to be confirmed, then the pope alone holds the key to the ordinary universal magisterium, since, without consulting the bishops, he could decide that the magisterium had pronounced itself on a given point and that this doctrine then belonged to its infallible magisterium.

---

43. Congregation for the Doctrine of the Faith, "[Instruction on] the Ecclesial Vocation of the Theologian," *Origins* 20 (July 5, 1990): 117, 119-126.

44. John Paul II, "Apostolic Letter *Motu proprio, Ad Tuendam Fidem*," *Origins* 28 (July 16, 1998): 113-116.

45. Some examples of truths belonging to the first category: the articles of the Creed, those dogmas which have been solemnly defined (Trinity, christology, grace, sacraments, etc.); belonging to the third: the diverse "authentic" teachings of the pope and the bishops (discourses, diverse documents, letters), that is to say, given by virtue of their office, but not in a definitive manner; from the second (new) category: the limiting of presbyterial ordination to men, the illicit character of euthanasia, prostitution, fornication, and also the legitimacy of a papal election or a council, and the canonization of saints.

Conclusion

227. The first chapter of this book helped us to gather together both the bright and dark aspects of our common heritage. More specifically, it recalled the early and medieval church's conviction of having received authority from Christ in doctrinal matters. As well, we noted significant historical development in the ways of organizing the communal, collegial, and personal dimensions of ecclesial life.

228. This second chapter lays before us two clearly divergent outlooks. The Reformation churches, reacting against certain medieval distortions, radically call into question the church's magisterial and hierarchical approach to doctrinal authority. They restore the primary authority of Scripture to its honored place and shift the concrete exercise of authority from hierarchical offices to the spiritual freedom of conscience and the responsibility of the whole community. At the same time, the Catholic Church increasingly accentuated the process of Roman centralization already begun in the Middle Ages. Nonetheless, behind these obvious divergences we discover a Christian consensus that is not to be minimized.

229. We must now bring together the complex lessons of history with the witness of Scripture. The Scriptures will provide us with criteria for discernment in the face of these vicissitudes and will help us to evaluate the calls to conversion that are being addressed to our respective churches.

CHAPTER THREE

Scripture: A Locus for Discernment in This Historical Journey

230. After this long journey through two millennia of ecclesial life, we now turn to Scripture, the primary and ultimate norm of our faith. This journey must be understood in the light of Scripture, in order to understand how it has been shaped by elements of both truth and distortions. As we did in our previous study on Mary, we can draw lessons from the interplay of history and Scripture that permit the formulation of a number of doctrinal propositions that might serve the reconciliation of the churches.

231. Our scriptural itinerary makes no claim to be a detailed exegetical analysis of each New Testament tradition. Neither does it claim to be an exhaustive study. It is essentially a biblical theology, that is to say, an identification of the lessons of faith that can be gathered concerning doctrinal authority in early Christian communities. More than amassing information, we seek to discern the main models of authority in the New Testament witness, and to grasp the dominating principle that cuts across and binds together the diverse books.

232. Our itinerary begins with the witness of the Synoptic Gospels, since they put us more directly in touch with the words and deeds of Jesus. The two related books, the Gospel of Luke and the Acts of the Apostles, will be treated together. Next, we will review the different strata of the Pauline corpus. Finally, we will consider the Johannine corpus.

Section I: The Synoptic Gospels

233. We will follow primarily the guiding thought of Matthew's Gospel, taking care to show points of agreement with the Gospels of Mark and Luke. We shall consider the personal authority of Jesus, the handing on of his authority to the disciples, taking note of the authority of the whole community and that of the Twelve respectively. Finally, we will consider what the Gospels say concerning the particular position of Peter.

I. The Sovereign Authority of Jesus

234. The term "authority" *(exousia)*[1] is almost always linked to the person of Jesus in Matthew's Gospel. He radiates a particular and original authority: the crowds attest to it (Matt. 7:28-29; see Mark 1:22), as do the pagan centurion (Matt. 8:8-9; see Luke 7:7-8), Jesus' compatriots (Matt. 13:54; see Mark 6:2), and the religious authorities (Matt. 21:23; see Mark 11:28).

235. Mark (see 1:27) and Matthew note that Jesus' authority is revealed through his teaching: in the Sermon on the Mount, Jesus proclaims the Kingdom of heaven, speaking as a master and not as a scribe (Matt. 7:29). On his own authority, Jesus proposes an interpretation of the Law of Moses that radicalizes and completes it, while contesting the rabbinical interpretation. Matthew underlines, even more than Mark, the fact that the authority of Jesus is linked to his teaching (compare, for example, Matt. 21:23 with Mark 11:28).

236. The authority of Jesus is underscored by the complete harmony between his word and his behavior: he does what he says and he says what he does; he lives as he teaches and he teaches as he lives. His proclamation of the gospel and his actions reveal the nearness of the Kingdom in a completely coherent manner. The charter of the Beatitudes is the charter of his own existence. During the temptation scenes, he forcefully rejects all selfish or easy options, the search for personal

---

1. The term *exousia* will always be translated in these pages by "authority," and not by "power," as is the case in many translations. The full authority of Jesus, received from the Father, grounds his capacity to exercise a force and a certain number of saving powers.

honor, and all desire for riches (Matt. 4:1-11). He renounces the possibility of making his authority into a power for its own sake, ordered to his own glory, or for constraining others.

237. At the same time, the authority of Jesus is expressed by his *acts of power* (Matt. 13:54). Indeed, there is an intimate relationship between the authority of his word and the miracles that follow from it, as recognized by the centurion (Matt. 8:8-9). Together they reveal that the reign of God is near and that this is Good News. Thus, they lead the crowds to follow Jesus (Matt. 4:23-25).

238. Finally, the authority of Jesus is revealed in *the forgiveness of sins:* "the Son of Man has authority on earth to forgive sins" (Matt. 9:6; see Mark 2:10). The accusation of blasphemy leveled by the scribes emphasizes that this is something that only God can do.

239. The source of Jesus' authority is an object of controversy (Matt. 21:23-27; see Mark 11:27-33; Luke 20:1-8). Where does it come from: from God or from the evil one? Jesus refuses to justify his authority, and freely chooses to keep silent. Yet the polemic that ensues shows in the end that his authority comes directly from God.

240. Mark emphasizes the authority of Jesus from the very beginning of his Gospel. Matthew wants to show that his authority is one of a kind. It differs from political domination, and is opposed to the authority of the scribes, the Pharisees, the elders, and the high priests. It comes from God's very self.

241. An analysis of the authority and power of Jesus cannot avoid a consideration of the cross. In his passion, Jesus is stripped of all power and abandoned to the whims of his adversaries. His authority is decisively revealed when he takes on our human weakness, and he faithfully lives his ministry right to the end. In his Servant witness he gives us the example of a "crucified authority," the model of all Christian authority.

II. The Handing on of Jesus' Authority to the Disciples

242. Jesus handed his authority on to his disciples. Matthew tells how Jesus chose the Twelve and gave them "authority" *(exousia)* over unclean spirits (Matt. 10:1; see Mark 6:7; Luke 9:1), demonstrating that his authority is, above all, a liberating authority. He sent this group out on mission to announce in words and deeds the news that the Kingdom of

heaven is near (Matt. 10:5-16). This first commissioning is related to the final scene of the Gospel.

243. The declaration of Matthew 18:18 is unique to this Gospel: "Whatever you bind on earth will be bound in heaven, and whatever you loose on earth will be loosed in heaven." This authority is conferred on the disciples, that is, on the community that the author has just dared to call "the church" (Matt. 18:17). This text is most likely referring not only to the forgiveness of sins, but also to a doctrinal authority pertaining to morals and the declaration of what is permitted or forbidden.

244. The final scene of Matthew's Gospel is a solemn act that affirms at once the fullness of authority belonging to the Risen Christ and the delegation of authority addressed to the Eleven.[2] Their authority is founded upon the legitimate authority of he who sends them out on mission with the triple imperative to make disciples, to baptize, and to teach, and on his promise of perpetual assistance. This mission is universal in space and time. The authority of the Eleven, or the symbolic group of the Twelve, is at once cultic (baptize) and doctrinal (teach). They receive it directly from the Lord, and not from the community.

III. The Authority of the Community and the Authority of the Twelve

245. Since the patristic era, exegetes have attempted to understand to whom exactly — to which persons and which institutions — the authority given by Jesus has been handed down. Matthew's Gospel tells us very little in this regard. Was he referring to the disciples in general, to the local church, to the Twelve, or to Peter? Many possible answers to this question would be relevant here. However, taken together, the expressions used by the Matthean redactor seem to indicate that he considers the community and its leaders from a synthetic point of view — that is, as a community that is not purely egalitarian, and within which there is a discernible authority structure.

246. The doctrinal authority which Jesus entrusted to the disciples therefore pertains to the whole community. Yet it does not ignore the unique role that belongs to the leaders represented in the symbolic im-

---

2. Judas is no longer among them.

age of the Twelve. The advice not to accept the title "Master," "Father," or "Teacher" presupposes the inherent temptation that comes with any responsibility, as does, "the greatest among you will be your servant" (Matt. 23:8-11). This is the Christian reversal of worldly authority (see Luke 22:24-27). The twenty-third chapter of Matthew's Gospel is not only aimed at the Pharisees; it also warns the community against acting in ways similar to those of the scribes (Matt. 23:34).

247. The Gospel's use of the term "church" presupposes the self-awareness of a community in which a function of judgment and authority is exercised. Matthew understands the church as a structured community, including persons who assume a specific authoritative role.

IV. The Figure of Peter and His Role

248. Lastly, the Gospel of Matthew highlights the image of Peter, even though he had already died by the time of its redaction.[3] This indicates that he was considered an important figure in the life of the church at that time. Peter certainly stands as a model of discipleship. Yet he plays an even greater role than this, for Matthew accords him a preeminent place in a series of texts of ecclesiological significance (Matt. 14:28-31; 15:15; 16:16-19; 17:24-27; 18:21). The evangelist presents Peter as an authoritative link between Jesus and the community.

249. The same evangelist underlines the human weakness of Peter. Matthew, like Mark, recounts his denials and the reproach of Jesus, who called him "Satan." Peter is at the same time both a man of little faith (Matt. 14:31) and the one who, thanks to God's gift, confesses the faith (16:17-18). The preeminence of Peter is based, not upon his personal qualities, but rather on the choice of the Lord.

250. In conclusion, for Matthew authority in the church is of secondary importance in relation to the authority of Christ. The latter authority, given and received, is at the service of the former. Further, the goal of doctrinal authority within the church is to foster the practice of Christian living. It is a service directed toward Christian life (see Matt. 20:28). It must be exercised in humility and fellowship.

---

3. The text of Matt. 16:17-19 was treated at length in our earlier document *Le ministère de communion dans l'Église universelle* (Paris: Le Centurion, 1986), nos. 96-107 and 127-129.

251. In contrast to Matthew who insists the upon Peter's importance,[4] Mark offers a model of bearing the gospel tradition without an apostolic figure. His account focuses on the inability of the disciples to understand the itinerary of their master in order to emphasize that Jesus alone can live the mystery of his particular calling. Similarly, he relates that fear prevented the women from announcing the resurrection in order to highlight the fact that the gospel could be handed on despite the limitations of the women and men who followed Jesus. While this is a different model of transmission, it does not contradict that of Matthew.

Section II: Doctrinal Authority in Luke and Acts

252. When he sends his disciples on mission for the first time, the Jesus of Luke's Gospel delegates his own authority — "Whoever listens to you listens to me" (Luke 10:16) — and entrusts them with the authority "to tread on snakes and scorpions, and over all the power of the enemy" (Luke 10:19). He also gives them the great commandment that guides all Christian authority and of which he himself is the greatest example: "the greatest among you must become like the youngest, and the leader like one who serves. . . . I am among you as one who serves" (Luke 22:26-27).

253. At the beginning of Acts, Luke takes up what Jesus said to his disciples in the final scene of his Gospel. He sends them out from Jerusalem as witnesses to the whole inhabited earth (Luke 24:47-48; Acts 1:8). The relationship of these two books thus reveals the manner in which Jesus' authority is handed on to the disciples. It is given to them by Jesus himself, and their authority is that of witnesses.

254. He who promises them this competence — Jesus, the Risen One — also tells them that this competence will be given to them when they receive the Holy Spirit (Acts 1:8). The gift of the Spirit at Pentecost, and throughout the account of Acts, fulfils this promise and gives concrete signs of its fruitfulness and universality.

255. The first of those who give witness are disciples who knew Jesus during his ministry (Acts 1:22), and their testimony concerns the resur-

---

4. In a similar fashion, the two later strata of the Pauline corpus (Colossians/Ephesians and the Pastorals) focus their attention on the authority of Paul, and the Johannine corpus on the anonymous figure of the beloved disciple.

rection. If the primary subject of their witness is the resurrection — for only the disciples saw the Risen Christ and can be called witnesses of the resurrection — they had to have known Jesus from the beginning in order to be an accredited witness and counted among the number of the apostles. For their witness consists in saying that the Risen One IS Jesus of Nazareth, a man known to everyone, and in revealing the coherence between his life and the reward of his resurrection.

256. The disciples vie with one another to underline the exclusive (he was revealed to us *alone*) and collegial (we are *all* witnesses) nature of their competence. The collegial dimension is essential, for it shows how their testimonies converge, and convergence and truth go together.

257. While in the beginning the only subject of their testimony is the resurrection — for the other events were known by all the inhabitants of Jerusalem and Judea, and the resurrection allowed them to understand their full meaning — it grew progressively to encompass the entire life of Jesus when it was addressed to listeners who only knew Jesus by hearsay.

258. This first witness was not the only one. In other words, the conditions of Acts 1:22 represent only a preliminary stage. For, without having known Jesus during his earthly life, Paul nevertheless becomes a witness accredited by God (spoken through the words of Ananias) and directly by Jesus himself, according to his vision (Acts 9:15, 18; 26:16). Paul is thus a truly accredited witness.

259. For the apostles who knew Jesus, as for Paul, the witness given to the Risen Christ presupposes the Spirit whose action is highlighted throughout Acts. It is the Spirit that enables the apostles to speak and act in the name of Jesus. Thanks to the Spirit, they are witnesses to the Risen Christ from Jerusalem to Rome.

260. Chapter 15 of Acts recounts how the Christian community quickly encountered conflict: should one require circumcision and the integral observance of the entire Mosaic Law of gentile converts? The apostles and elders gathered to consider this matter and "there was much debate" (Acts 15:6-7). In the end, it was "with the consent of the whole church," through a collegial deliberation and decision, that they were able to bring the crisis to an end. Their final decision, taken in the communion of the Spirit — "for it has seemed good to the Spirit and to us" (Acts 15:28) — reveals a concern to preserve "the truth of the gospel"

(see Gal. 2:14) and, at the same time, to respect the traditions of different groups. The main point is that even in their diverse practices, Christians shared the experience of being saved by the grace of the Lord Jesus (see Acts 15:11).

261. Whereas the first part of Acts is dominated by the figure of Peter, the second part is dominated by that of Paul. Luke reports his intensive preaching and evangelizing activity throughout the Mediterranean Basin. Paul's testimony fundamentally concerns his vision of the Risen One. One might say this is a narrow focus. Perhaps, but he witnesses to the radical change brought about by this encounter. His witness to Christ is certainly no substitute for the testimony of those who know Jesus during his ministry. Paul extends the experience and confirms it by locating it within a personal history transformed by the encounter with the Risen Christ. A witness can only testify to the encounter at the heart of his own existence. For Paul, giving witness means recounting how the Risen One changed his life and conformed it to his own. In this regard, his testimony inaugurates the witness of a generation (ours) that did not know the earthly Jesus, but knows only the Risen Christ. Through him our lives become the place where his truth and power are revealed. The content, the authority, the truth, and the influence of Paul's testimony (and of the generation he represents) are thus set down at the end of the book of Acts (Acts 21-28).

Section III: The Pauline Epistles and the Pauline Literature

I. The First Letters of Paul

262. The authority to which all must submit is that of the gospel, for it comes from God. The gospel is authoritative because it liberates, saves, and grants the believer the status as a child of God.

263. The proclamation of the gospel provokes new questions for which Jesus had not given an answer. For example, he said nothing concerning the status of men and women of non-Jewish origin who would come to believe in him. It was therefore up to Jesus' disciples to discern the place of Gentile believers within their midst: should they become Jews to have full access to salvation, or was circumcision foreign to the gospel?

264. As the apostle to the nations, Paul is confronted directly by this question. It forced him to reflect on the ecclesial consequences of the gospel message. In saying that circumcision did not belong to the gospel, he declares his position not only concerning the status of Gentile Christians, but also concerning the status of ecclesial group. Paul's discourse concerning the church flows directly from his reflection on the gospel (see 1 Cor. 1-4). This is why submitting to the gospel means respecting the principle of Christ as the unique Savior in its ultimate consequences.

265. The Scriptures of the Old Testament are also authoritative — having an authority that is prophetic and is directed toward the gospel. The principle of the Pauline reading of the Scriptures refers them immediately to Christ and to the salvation he brings. It is the gospel — and faith in the gospel — that opens the mind to understand the Scriptures and enables us to grasp their orientation, and thus, their authority (see Rom. 9; 2 Cor. 3).

266. Paul makes high claims for himself as having the authority of an apostle who has been "set apart" (Rom. 1:1) within the context of the gospel, "called to be an apostle of Christ Jesus by the will of God" (1 Cor. 1:1; 2 Cor. 1:1) and not "from human authorities" (Gal. 1:1). His apostolic authority comes from having been chosen to announce the gospel.

267. As essential as it may be, the choice of God is not sufficient. It is by living the gospel, in other words, because one can read the gospel in his life, that the apostle is a true witness to the gospel (see 1 Cor. 4:9-15). Identified with his Lord, his very life reveals the newness of the gospel. This authority is recognized in the very fruits of the gospel, through the growth of communities in faith, hope, and love.

268. Paul dares to apply the term *letter* to the Corinthians: "You yourselves are our letter, written on our hearts, to be known and read by all; and you show that you are a letter of Christ, prepared by us, not written with ink but with the Spirit of the living God, not on tables of stone but on tablets of human hearts" (2 Cor. 3:2-3). This letter of accreditation comes from the Spirit not only in its origin, but also in its addressees. It establishes the legitimacy of Paul's ministry, which is confirmed by the fruit it bears and attested by the Corinthians' faith. Having received Paul's teaching, the Corinthians have become a letter of recommendation for all his actions. The *reception* of doctrinal authority becomes, in turn, its expression.

269. Paul is absolutely committed to remaining in communion with the college of the apostles at Jerusalem, whom he calls "pillars," "to make sure that I was not running . . . in vain" (Gal. 2:2). This communion endured the conflict with Peter, to ensure that the church was "acting consistently with the truth of the gospel" (Gal. 2:14) of justification by faith in Christ and not by the works of the law, a gospel in which there is no longer Jew nor Greek (Gal. 3:28). Engaging in a vigorous dialogue, which did not exclude moments of opposition, the apostles saw through the crisis and remained united in their preaching.

270. Concerning the doctrine of marriage, Paul makes a clear distinction between what he commands because it is "not I but the Lord" (1 Cor. 7:10), and what he advises — "I say — I and not the Lord" (v. 12). This distinction is worth noting, for not every exercise of authority in the church has the same weight.

271. The apostle's authority is brought to bear on the celebration of the Lord's Supper. This meal of sharing and of communion is not to be contradicted by the egotism of a meal where "one goes away hungry and another becomes drunk" (1 Cor. 11:21), that is, where a mockery is made of communal charity.

272. Lastly, the authority of Paul reveals the power of Christ at work in the midst of his own human weakness: "I will boast all the more gladly of my weaknesses, so that the power of Christ may dwell in me" (2 Cor. 12:9-10). In this he is conformed to the self-emptying *(kenosis)* of Christ who was "crucified in weakness, but lives by the power of God" (2 Cor. 13:4).

273. While Paul attempts to convince his listeners by arguing with authority, it is never his intention to arbitrarily impose his convictions on them. Rather, he draws attention to their own inner experience of the love that God has for them in Jesus Christ. He never forgets that the Christian comes to the point of judgment and decision because the Spirit moves them from within (Phil. 3:15). Though he insists upon his own apostolic authority, he also reminds the early Christian communities of their proper authority — a collective authority — over disciplinary questions that have important doctrinal implications (1 Cor. 5:4-5). Indeed, throughout his letters Paul shows how halachic[5] problems are

---

5. *Halacha* is the rule governing practical behavior and the official guide for daily life in Judaism.

related to questions concerning the truth and purity of the gospel. This is why institutional authority and doctrinal authority are inseparable in his eyes, as he indicates in the Letter to the Galatians.

II. The Letters to the Colossians and to the Ephesians

274. The letters to the Colossians and to the Ephesians explicitly address the question of the ongoing role of doctrinal authority. By saying that the *mysterion* was revealed to the "holy apostles and prophets" (Eph. 3:5) they present the former as the trustees of the gospel message. It is not that we must repeat their teaching, but the proclamation of the gospel throughout history retains the testimony of the first apostles and prophets as its point of reference. In this way, the gospel will always preserve its apostolic character, as something that was revealed to the apostles.

275. As in the previous epistles, authority must be exercised in the church (Eph. 5:2), in mutual submission (Eph. 5:21), and in the imitation of Christ who has loved us and has laid down his life for us.

III. The Pastoral Letters

276. The theology of the Pastorals is expressed in the relationship between exhortation and the proclamation of salvation that warrants it. Largely determined by conflict with those who "teach different doctrine" (1 Tim. 1:3), this proclamation is presented as a *sound teaching* and a *good treasure*, a faithful handing on of Paul's teaching (1 Tim. 1:19; 6:20; 2 Tim. 2:12, 14; Titus 1:9). It not only makes use of traditions, it claims to be *the* tradition.

277. Paul is presented as the necessary path to the proclamation of salvation, the center of its correct transmission. The conflict with his adversaries is a dispute among teachers concerning the matter of knowledge. In the face of useless pursuits and endless genealogies (1 Tim. 1:4; 2 Tim. 2:23; Titus 1:14; 3:9), the Pastorals attempt to draw a line to the present community from its origin in God. The knowledge of salvation is not esoteric, its line of transmission is clear. From the beginning God had willed the salvation of humanity. This decision,

which became a reality revealed in Christ, is contained in the message
entrusted to Paul (1 Tim. 1:11ff.; 2:6ff.; 2 Tim. 1:9ff; Titus 1:1-4). Paul reminds Timothy and Titus that salvation is the ultimate motivation of
the *good treasure* and of the *sound teaching* (1 Tim. 1:10; 2 Tim. 4:3; Titus
1:9; 2:1). In turn, Timothy and Titus would have to choose just persons
to continue teaching (1 Tim. 2:2). Outside of this communicative gene-
alogy, whose origin is controlled — *good treasure, sound teaching* — is
found the vain pursuit of error.

278. Paul precedes other believers and ministers as a justified sinner and as a teacher. At the same time, on judgment day he will still be
the model of the responsible Christian rewarded with those who have
longed with love for the epiphany of the Lord (2 Tim. 4:8). He is also the
prototype of the faithful believer in the continuity of a family tradition
(2 Tim. 1:3). Finally, Paul is a model of those who suffer for their preaching of the gospel (2 Tim. 1:12; 2:9), yet are already victorious (2 Tim.
4:18). He himself has passed through all the steps of the course outlined in the exhortation.

279. Yet Paul is no longer with the Christian community (1 Tim.
3:14; 4:13f.). The stretching of the present moment — with its delay and
waiting — demands a significant attention to the social dimension of
the community. "The house of God," the church, becomes an object of
exhortation. The way in which the community affirms its living bond
with the apostle in his absence is by behaving in "the house of God" in
accord with Paul's instructions. The practice of ministry takes up
where he left off. Ordination, family education, teaching, exhortation,
and suitable behavior are the contemporary equivalent to the action
once accomplished by the apostle when Timothy listened to his words
and shared in his "adventures." The mandate of Timothy and Titus reflects the outline of present ministerial tasks that began with Paul's
journey.

280. Paul's directives do not supply a map of individual progress in
the virtues or in moral and philosophical qualities. They are addressed
to a *community leader* located in a fully institutional space. Timothy is
called in view of his *role,* theologically designated as "servant of Jesus
Christ" (1 Tim. 4:6), "man of God" (1 Tim. 6:11; 2 Tim. 3:17), and "servant
of the Lord" (2 Tim. 2:24). His authority, which comes from the apostle,
is validated *by the established community,* as he is constantly reminded
(1 Tim. 4:14; 6:12; 2 Tim. 2:19-21; 3:10-17). It is *for the community* that he is

to conform to the instructions he has received (1 Tim. 4:6, 10, 12, 16; 2 Tim. 2:23; 3:12; Titus 3:8, 14).

281. The flow of communication which has its beginning and end in God the Savior, and goes out from and returns to the community, risks being interrupted by *the adversaries*. The Pastoral Letters respond to this danger by outlining the role of the minister in the strongest of terms. They are rooted in the Pauline tradition and depict the scene of that faithful transmission from Paul to his two disciples. The importance ascribed to the image of the recipient provides the ministry with its motivation and its norm. At the outset the gospel was entrusted to the apostle (1 Tim. 1:11 and parallels), and while he is absent the task is to be carried on. He himself establishes the norm for ministry, and ensures that his instructions are passed on and that others will be present to carry them out. Every minister should consider themselves a disciple of Paul by the same right as Timothy and Titus. Through a whole series of relationships to the community, to God, to the world, to the Pauline sources, and against the enemies of the faith, the *form of the leader's role* begins to take shape. Its depth and temporal weight correspond to the church conceived as a household of God.

282. The qualities required by the minister, episkopos, or deacon (1 Tim. 3:1-13), "God's steward" (Titus 1:7), are the same as those required of any steward, of any honest man in the society of the day. What is said of the episkopos is also said of the deacon or the presbyter, and in part of widows and all believers. The particular profile of the Christian leader, called to take his place as "coordinator" in the "house of God," takes shape in relation to the different spaces of the community's life.

283. From a social point of view, the episkopos seems to be the head of the household. Anyone without family ties and living as an itinerant preacher would not likely be taken into consideration as a community leader, as there was concern for the stability and consolidation of the church. Ethically speaking, the private life of the episkopos was in harmony with the accepted norms of the day. If the episkopos was the master of the house, he fulfilled this role as God's representative, as a steward (Titus 1:7). The "master" of the large house, who is at once present and absent, is the Lord (2 Tim. 2:21).

284. A certain experience of the faith over time is essential (see Titus 1:9: "firm grasp"). Thus, in choosing an episkopos, the direction

that "he must not be a recent convert" (1 Tim. 3:6) establishes a negative criterion for one who has not spent sufficient time in the community. The pride that might tempt a newly converted Christian if he were promoted too quickly is linked to the danger of heresy: not being well rooted in his new faith, he is more fragile. This concern is reflected in the procedure for choosing *deacons*. They must first be tested and prove themselves (1 Tim. 3:10). Similarly, in the case of *presbyters*, none are to receive the laying on of hands too hastily (1 Tim. 5:22). This concern with long experience and continuity does not preclude an exhortation to give special consideration to the young leader (1 Tim. 4:12), provided that he has been educated in the faith from childhood.

285. Good reputation appears as the decisive criterion of selection: "he must be well thought of by outsiders" (1 Tim. 3:7; 5:14; 6:1; Titus 2:5; 2:8, 10). Exemplary conduct remains a *distinctive* sign which even outsiders find *readable*. The episkopos represents the community to society. Ministers are to be blameless and respectable in all things, as can be attested by their domestic lives.

286. Ministry takes form in three spaces: the community understood as an enlarged household — and closely related to it, the private home and society. If the internal harmony of the community conveys a message to the wider society, the private home, where the daily ethic of any "honest man" or woman is proven, also offers a place to confirm the conduct of the responsible Christian.

287. The text of Titus 1:9 clearly assigns the task of combating adversaries to the episkopos; the profile of the minister is presented as their antithesis. If there is a debate with the adversaries concerning the meaning of the present time — "the resurrection has already taken place" (2 Tim. 2:18) — the profile of the minister suggests that the conflict also concerns the order and the disorder of places and spaces. The minister must express in his daily living the correct relationship between the different spaces mentioned (home, church, and society). The adversaries, who disrupt households, seem to call these relationships into question directly or indirectly. Failures in the domestic sphere may well lead to a dangerous deterioration in societal relationships.

288. The blueprint of the Pastorals demands a significant teaching effort from community leaders. The teaching function of the episkopos, who knows how to oppose the teaching of false teachers with "sound teaching," is central to his role as the leader of the com-

munity (1 Tim. 3:2; 5:17; Titus 1:9). Moreover, the Pastorals are not alone in this view at a time — during Christianity's third generation — when communities were confronted with two problems: the spread of heretical doctrines and the disappearance of prophecy.

289. The reason for teaching is one of the constant themes of these letters. "Grace," itself instructive (Titus 2, 12), is the theological motive for the pedagogical function of ministry. The authority necessary for this task rests on apostolicity, on the "Pauline" character of exhortations understood to continue the heritage of the apostles against unfounded interpretations. The important thing is that the norms of the apostle, who in the final analysis is Christ himself (1 Tim. 6:13f.), are maintained. Thus, the direction of a community does not base its authority on tasks indicated by the community, or that it delegates to someone. Rather, it is grounded in the apostolic norm which is itself founded on the gospel. The minister comes from the community and exercises his or her responsibility within the community. Nonetheless, ministry is not a function of the community, it is a "service" *(diakonia)*. It answers to the Lord of the church, of which it is the steward.

Section IV: The Johannine Writings

290. *(Reference to Christ)* The intention of the Fourth Gospel is not the establishment of the church, but rather the proclamation of salvation accomplished in Christ and the call to live in faith, a faith that is truly the source of life (John 20:30-31). Hence, it is not surprising that the vocabulary of authority *(exousia)* appears in relation to the mission exercised by Jesus. It is not a matter of discretionary authority exercised in the manner of human governments (see the dialogue with Pilate in 19:10-11). Rather, it is a qualification received personally from the Father, according to a logic of gift that implies, not a power over others, but a capacity to give oneself completely (17:1-2): "No one takes [my life] from me, but I lay it down of my own accord. I have power to lay it down, and I have power to take it up again. I have received this command from my Father" (10:18).

291. Vested with full authority (image of the seal, John 6:27), the Son — sent by the Father — has the capacity to exercise the role of the eschatological judge (figure of the Son of Man, 5:27). This refers less to

a trial in the juridical sense of the word, than it does to the discernment carried out in the heart of the human person, a process marked by both light and darkness (3:19-21). The plan of God is fully salvific (3:16-17). Welcoming the incarnate Word confers on believers the status of children of God with the authority appertaining to this filial condition: "But to all who believed in his name, he gave power to become children of God" (1:12).

292. *(Reference to the Church)* While the convictions of the Fourth Gospel concerning Christ are strong and assured, the same cannot be said regarding the church. Modern research has uncovered the difficulties encountered by the Johannine community as it confronted several major crises: the break from Judaism, concretized in a painful measure of excommunication from the synagogue (John 9:22; 12:42; 16:2); disenchantment with the world, with a pagan society incapable of adherence to Christ (chapters 15–18); and internal divisions after serious disagreements on christological matters (1 John 2:18-19; 4:2-3).

293. Compelled to envisage two concrete modes for the exercise of authority, the Johannine community found itself divided between:

- an unconditional attachment to the beloved disciple, authentic witness to the whole paschal mystery (washing of the feet, John 13:23-26; crucifixion, 19:26-27; empty tomb, 20:8) and guarantor of the truth of the Johannine witness (19:35) beyond his own death (21:21-24);
- the awareness of the presbyter, responsible for the community in the period of the epistles, of belonging simultaneously to a collective body acting in a collegial manner (the multiple use of "we" in 1 John) and to a confessing tradition, rooted in the paschal event and handed on through the witness of several generations of believers (1 John 1:1-4).

294. At the last supper the beloved disciple was so close to Jesus that he became the necessary intermediary between Jesus and the other disciples, beginning with Peter (John 13:23-26). Moreover, at the foot of the cross the beloved disciple was accorded the role of brother and heir of Jesus — "Here is your mother" (19:27) — which bestowed on him a delegation of authority over the community. The example given by Jesus in the washing of the feet constitutes an essential reference for the

exercise of ecclesial authority. Such authority can only be service — "For I have set you an example, that you should do as I have done to you" (13:15) — and can never take the place of him alone, who, as "the way, the truth and the life," can lead us to the Father (14:6).

295. In the end, the Johannine community seems to have accepted the necessity of an ecclesiological model that is built upon more than the reference to the authority of the founding disciple alone. It did so without renouncing its proper tradition (John 21:24). The rehabilitation of Peter, surrounded by the halo of the glory of martyrdom (21:15-19), reflects the desire of the Johannine group to establish bonds of communion with other communities whose institutional models were different from its own.

296. *(Reference to the Spirit)* On several occasions the gift of the Paraclete Spirit is presented as the direct consequence of Jesus' departure (John 14:15-18, 26; 15:26-27; 16:7). The Spirit is thus inseparable from the post-Easter reality. It exercises a teaching and revelatory function among believers, permitting the reception and actualization of the words of Jesus (15:26; 16:12-15). From this time on, each disciple is called to accomplish works that are equal or even superior to those of Jesus (14:12).

297. The authority of the Holy Spirit is invoked in the midst of ecclesial difficulties, not only to legitimize but doubtless also to regulate the community discipline of excommunication and the reintegration of those members guilty of serious violations. On the evening of Easter, the message of the Risen Christ to the disciples is a commissioning: "As the Father has sent me, so I send you" (John 20:21). Yet the gift of his breath is especially aimed at defining the frontiers of a community concerned with the truth in the maintenance of its identity: "When he had said this, he breathed on them and said to them, 'Receive the Holy Spirit. If you forgive the sins of any, they are forgiven them; if you retain the sins of any, they are retained'" (20:22-23).

298. If, then, in Johannine theology authority belongs first to the Son sent by the Father, it continues to act through the gift of the Spirit in an actual community that is compelled to act with authority in difficult situations. In such circumstances, the Holy Spirit carries out its mission of "Counselor" reflected in the juridical title (Paraclete/advocate) conferred by the Fourth Gospel.

299. *(Reference to the Believer)* While recognizing the necessity of an ecclesial institution associated with the authority of the Lord, through

the working of the Spirit the Johannine community affirms the relative autonomy of the believing subject. In the midst of crisis, the first epistle dares to assert, "you do not need anyone to teach you" (1 John 2:27). To justify such an affirmation, the author appeals to the "anointing" received from the Holy One (2:20) who "teaches you about all things" (2:27).

300. No matter what the effect of the Spirit or of the Word, this anointing (*charisma* in Greek) constitutes the mark of adherence to Christ inscribed in every believer. Theoretically, it ought to inspire a correct discernment of what is true and false in christological matters (1 John 4:1-6) and render useless the exercise of a teaching ministry. However, the utopian character of such a position departs from the twenty-first chapter of the Gospel which both appeals to the authority of the beloved disciple (John 21:24) and justifies recourse to the figure of Peter (21:15-19).

301. From this tension internal to Johannine theology emerges the strong conviction according to which each disciple first receives his proper identity from the close relationship he maintains with Christ. Like the branches abiding in the vine (John 15:1-7), like the sheep that are all known personally by the shepherd and who survive only by passing through the one door (10:1-18), believers form one people to the extent that each receives their identity totally and personally from the one Lord. The reference to Christ thus constitutes the point of equilibrium between an insistence on the legitimate authority of the beloved disciple and the egalitarian dimension linked to the active presence of the Spirit.

Section V: The Canon of the New Testament

302. Without claiming to be exhaustive, our study of the principal New Testament texts confirms a diversity of models relative to the exercise of doctrinal authority in the post-Easter communities. The figures proposed by Matthew, Luke, Paul, and John present different emphases. Within each of these four traditions there are also tensions. It would be tempting to favor one book to the detriment of the others, considering them less important in this matter.

303. The establishment of the New Testament canon, following a

long process of mutual recognition on the part of the churches and diverse communities, had the effect not only of linking the different books but of according, *de facto,* the same normative value to each. This does not mean, however, that the differences between the models of authority proposed by the different books are to be ignored. One could say that the canon of Scripture already constitutes a good example of differentiated consensus. A common reference to the unique sovereign authority of Christ in fact assures the unity among the diverse conceptualizations and ecclesial practices of authority, to the extent that differences of all kinds affect the communities' lifestyle.

304. The recognition of the biblical canon, especially of the New Testament canon, testifies to the authority of Scripture over the church and for the church. At the same time, it is a communal act through which the churches recognize their solidarity with one another through sharing in one faith. For those writings which held what were perceived as real doctrinal differences were not received into the canon.

Conclusions regarding Scripture

305. At the conclusion of this overview, we wish to gather together the main points that ought to direct the next step of our research on doctrinal authority. First, we note an obvious diversity in the manner of presenting and grounding authority in the witness of the New Testament traditions. Yet, by receiving them into the canon, the post-apostolic church read them as forming a real unity.

306. (The Authority of Jesus) *The gospel stories insist on the authority that Jesus receives from the Father, from the beginning of his public life. This authority is that of proclaiming the Kingdom of God, the mystery of which is revealed in the coherence between Jesus' words and acts of liberation, healing, and forgiveness.*

307. Jesus receives authority from God his Father in view of his mission to proclaim the coming reign of God and the salvation of humanity by his words and deeds. In his way of exercising it, Jesus gives an example of an authority of pure service, an authority directed toward the gift of salvation.

308. (Authority That Is Handed On) *Jesus remains present in the age of the church, albeit according to another modality. He maintains all authority over the church, though it is no longer exercised through his visible presence. For, at Easter, he entrusted this authority to his disciples. He delegated it to them as if to a group of trustees. He truly gives it to them without abandoning or letting go of it. Authority exercised in the church is always a form of stewardship which points back to the one Master and Lord, who is at once present and absent in the church. In the power of the Spirit, authority is exercised by the disciples in truth following the example of their Lord.*

309. This authority is conferred in several ways. It was first communicated to those who knew Jesus, then to others such as Paul. With time it reached the disciples and communities of subsequent generations, giving rise to diverse institutional structures of ministry.

310. The post-apostolic church receives its authority from the apostolic church, a fact to which the letters to the Colossians, Ephesians, and the Pastorals testify in particular.[6] Thus, the post-apostolic church declares the necessity of submitting to the gospel handed down by the apostles. Despite their death, the church remains apostolic and retains this definitive characteristic.

311. (The Exercise of Authority) This process does not take place without passing through diverse crises witnessed in the New Testament writings, including questions such as the confrontation between Peter and Paul, the problem of knowing whether Jewish observances ought to be imposed on Gentile Christians, and legitimizing leaders after the disappearance of the first witnesses. The New Testament also indicates the means for dealing with crises through a continual return to the gospel.

312. For the New Testament, authority takes the form of service (diakonia) *not only in the person of Christ, but also in the person of all those who are entrusted with responsibility in the church.*

313. The New Testament affirms not only the authority of Scripture (referring back to the Old Testament), but also that of the words of those who witness the event of Jesus Christ — words which are concretized in the redaction of New Testament, of the confessions of faith, and of the first liturgies. We also note the emergence of a typology of persons vested with authority (the witness, the prophet, the disciple . . .) and the affirmation that this authority is handed on following the death of the first witnesses. Lastly, we note the active and responsible role of the communities. In short, the New Testament describes a first functioning of diverse structures in the exercise of authority — personal, collegial, and communal. On the basis of the orientations given in the New Testament concerning the functioning of authority, we can discern models that may help us in the exercise of authority in the church of our day.

---

6. The same orientation can be found in the catholic epistles and in chapter 21 of the Gospel of John.

CHAPTER FOUR

Doctrinal Proposals

314. In the first three parts of this study we gathered together, with care and respect, many facts that will remain at the center of our attention. We have been doing "anamnesis." In what follows, we wish to make a contribution through our group's engagement with the difficult question of doctrinal authority in the church. We hope this new chapter will be considered as "therapeutic."

315. In the first part of this chapter we will attempt to speak together, identifying areas that can be considered as the object of consensus between our churches. We acknowledge that the area of consensus can be at once shared and *differentiated*[1] due to our different traditions and respective practices (I). Following that we shall treat the differences that remain between us, calmly and with lucidity, within the framework of our consensus concerning the authority of the gospel over the church (II). Finally, we shall make several proposals aimed at encouraging the conversion of these differences and broadening the area of consensus (III). The chapter is structured according to a progression of these three steps.

---

1. We use the word *differentiated* in the same sense that it is given in the Lutheran-Roman Catholic *Joint Declaration on the Doctrine of Justification,* signed at Augsburg, October 31, 1999. It affirms a basic agreement in the truths of the faith concerning Jesus Christ, Savior, and justification by faith, etc. This consensus on basic truths covers and includes a certain number of *differences* that, in light of the consensus, can now be considered only as *divergences* [i.e., no longer church-dividing. — Trans.].

Section I: A Differentiated Consensus

316. In order to understand the "differentiated consensus" that emerges from our ecclesial practices, it is necessary to consider the authority of *texts*, of *persons*, the role of *institutional structures*, and finally, the problems raised by their functioning. Of course, all authority "binds," that is to say, it both compels and links one to the gospel. We are mindful that there is a hierarchy among the diverse forms of doctrinal authority. Lastly, we must take account not only of instances of authority in the past, but also of those in the present which open us to future horizons of faith.

1. The Authority of Texts

317. The authoritative texts of the Christian faith include the following: first and above all the *Scriptures,* then *the confessions of faith, creedal and doctrinal documents of the great councils, liturgies, catechisms, disciplinary texts,* and certain *ecumenical documents.* There are obviously different degrees of authority among these diverse texts, which cannot all be considered on the same level.

318. Together we confess the *sovereign authority of the Holy Scriptures.* We acknowledge their value as the ultimate norm *(norma normans)* for the faith of Christians. For in them we receive the authentic testimony of the Word of God and of the gospel. All other authoritative discourses of faith *(norma normata)* must be measured against the witness of the Scriptures. According to the very logic of the incarnation, the revelation of God reaches the believer through the expression of a human word. This involvement of what comes from God in the Holy Spirit and that which comes from humanity in the expression of faith will characterize every exercise of authority in the church at different levels.

This proclamation of the authority of the Scriptures was put into practice in the third chapter of this study where we attempted to confirm the basis for the exercise of doctrinal authority in the church through the Scriptures. Through the active recognition of this ultimate norm, we intend to compose our doctrinal proposals.

319. We recognize the authority of *confessions of faith.* These origi-

nate in the New Testament itself.[2] They possess both a confessing and a doctrinal value. Their role is to bring together the essential or the central message of the Scriptures into brief, structured formulas. They are a major expression of the tradition of faith.

320. There is a give-and-take of mutual interpretation between the confessions of faith and the Scriptures. The church summarizes the abundant diversity of the pages of Scripture in the unity of the confession, which appears as the grammar and the essential content of its message. For its part, the confession of faith only has meaning when considered in light of the priority of Scripture. In this sense one can say that the confessions interpret the Scriptures and that, on the other hand, Scripture remains the normative criterion for the interpretation of the confessions which exist to serve it. The confessions offer a synthesis of the Scriptures at a given time and as a reflection of a given culture, while the Scriptures call the churches of all times through their confessions of faith.

321. This is especially true of the early confessions such as the Apostles' Creed. Even though the apostles did not write it themselves, the churches of the West received it as vested with an apostolic authority. Similarly, the churches of the East and West received the creed of Nicaea-Constantinople as the renewed expression of the faith of the apostles in a period where the trinitarian faith was called into question. As well, the definition of Chalcedon constitutes a christological confession of faith, even though it has never enjoyed a liturgical status.

322. The confessions of the Modern period, written by the churches born in the divisions of the sixteenth century (for example, the confessions of Augsburg and La Rochelle, for Lutheran and Reformed Christians), respond to the same need. They also served to define and confirm the respective identity of these churches, and the demands of common witness for a given context (see The Barmen Declaration of 1934, or the confession of the Presbyterian Church of South Africa in 1973[3]).

2. Jesus is given a title: Rom. 10:9; Phil. 2:11; 1 Cor. 12:3; Acts 18:5 and 28; 1 John 2:22; Acts 8:36-38. Jesus died and is risen: 1 Cor. 15:3-5; Acts 2:14-39 (kerygma); Jesus has come in the flesh: 1 John 4:2; 2 John 7. Binary formulas, God and Christ: 1 Cor. 8:6; 1 Tim. 2:5-6. Threefold model, Father, Son, Spirit: 1 Cor. 12:4-6; Eph. 4:4-6.

3. The 1934 Barmen Declaration formally opposed the positions of the "German Christians" who were tempted to submit to certain Nazi ideas. The South African con-

323. Together we recognize and give priority to the *first four ecumenical councils*,[4] for their decisions enabled the churches to remain in the authenticity of faith at times when it was in peril. Certain points of the apostolic message became the object of a *status confessionis*. That is to say, the decisions taken in their regard were judged to be decisive from the perspective of communion in the same faith. The authority of the councils was exercised for the benefit of fidelity to the truth, as it is recorded in the Scriptures. For this reason the celebration of a council was considered a new Pentecost.

324. Since the separations of the fifth, eleventh, and sixteenth centuries, each church has continued to ensure the handing on and regulation of the faith through the documents of councils, synods, and creeds. These documents are norms submitted to the authority of the Scriptures *(norma normata)*. The degree of their authority varies with each document. It depends on the manner in which the assembly or the person who issued the accompanying edict intended to be bound by it. Since the time of separation, the reference of these dogmatic, synodal, and creedal texts is no longer the same for all the churches. This raises a future problem concerning the nature of the bond of fidelity to these texts that each church considers necessary.

325. In the name of the traditional principle, *the rule of prayer is the rule of faith (lex orandi, lex credendi)*, we recognize that *liturgies* — which are a prayed dimension of the interpreters of Scripture — form part of the identity of the churches, for which they signify and bring about communion. The great baptismal, eucharistic, and other liturgies are authoritative documents for the expression of faith.

326. The early church handed on its faith to adult catechumens through a *catechesis,* most often developed on the basis of a baptismal confession of faith. In the course of history, the catechesis of adults continued through the use of *catechisms*. These were developed for both adults and children. The sixteenth century was an important period for the flourishing of such texts in both the Reformation churches and in

---

fession of faith fought against the racist system of apartheid. In these two cases, burning questions were raised up to the level of a *status confessionis,* that is to say, a criteria of faith in discerning what is Christian from what is not.

4. Namely, Nicaea (325), Constantinople I (381), Ephesus (431), and Chalcedon (451). It should not be forgotten that the Oriental Orthodox Churches do not recognize the fourth council.

the Catholic Church. The catechetical texts which have been handed down and used by the churches are also important documents of faith.

327. In the series of authoritative texts under consideration, we should not forget *juridical documents*, whether they have a broad application as, in the Catholic Church, does the *Code of Canon Law* for the Western Church, or the *Code of Canons of the Eastern Churches*. Other documents have more of a regional scope, as do texts called *Discipline, Constitution, Agenda,* or *Articles* in the Reformation churches. The homology between these texts is real, even if they are not of the same order. These juridical documents are not simply regulations. They aim to put faith into practice in the pastoral and communal aspects of Christian life. They are authoritative and constitute doctrinal points of reference.

328. Today we are witnessing the emergence of a new type of authoritative documents, the *documents of ecumenical agreement* (for example, the *Leuenberg Accord* between the Reformed and Lutheran Churches of Europe,[5] the *Joint Declaration on the Doctrine of Justification* between the churches of the Lutheran World Federation and the Roman Catholic Church, and the common affirmation of Reuilly[6]). Whenever two or more churches are able to subscribe together to a declaration expressing their agreement in faith, and together draw practical consequences from it (as with the *Ecumenical Charter*[7]), this means, no matter what the extent of their agreement, that they each recognize the authority of what has been agreed. Given the recent character of these documents, their reception is still underway and the exact degree of their authority will only become clear in the future.

329. Can the authority of written documents suffice? No, for the

5. An agreement signed in 1973 between Lutheran, Reformed, and United Churches in Europe which established full communion with regard to preaching and the administration of the sacraments. Since 2003, this communion is called the Communion of European Protestant Churches.

6. A declaration signed in 2001 by the Anglican churches of Great Britain and Ireland and the Lutheran and Reformed churches of France. It established visible unity in regard to preaching and the sacraments, including reciprocal Eucharistic hospitality. It does not, however, permit the interchangeability of ministers. See *Appelés à témoigner et à servir* (Paris: Les Bergers et les Mages, 1999).

7. A document signed in Strasbourg in 2001 by representatives of the Conference of European Churches (KEK) and the Council of European Episcopal Conferences (CCEE) setting down "guidelines in view of increasing collaboration among the churches in Europe." See "Charta Oecumenica," http://www.cec-kek.org/content/charta.html.

simple reason that the text only takes its meaning within a living community that recognizes itself as bound by it. This is the sense of the early determination of the canon of Scripture. Moreover, every text requires the constant work of interpretation through time, carried on through both the personal and communal Christian consciousness, and by institutional authorities.

330. The preceding review of texts that have been received as authoritative demonstrates clearly that the very process of handing them on is part of the phenomenon of interpretation which is continually renewed as a function of questions arising in society, culture, and history. In our time, these include secularization, the pursuit of ecumenical dialogue, Jewish-Christian dialogue, and inter-religious debates. This same need applies equally to the text of Scripture, if the Christian community is not to content itself with the repetition of empty words.

The authority of texts leads us then to a consideration of the authority of the communities and persons who produce them.

2. The Authority of Communities and Persons

331. It goes without saying that the texts that we recognize as authoritative do not exist in isolation. As texts, they are a letter, and can easily become a dead letter. They exist within the dynamic of ecclesial life animated by the Spirit of God, and find their meaning within a community of persons. The living gospel that touches human hearts, inspires faith, converts, and justifies has been entrusted to a people in a handing on that can be traced back to the preaching of the apostles. In their wake the early church fathers represent an indispensable example of that handing on. They practiced a living and contemporary reading of Scripture in service of their communities and in dialogue with questions raised by the culture and social life of their time. In this way, the Scriptures are entrusted to the church that guards them faithfully, and is preserved and ordered by them.

332. We now come to a consideration of the communities and persons considered as authoritative in the realm the faith: *the living tradition of faith, the authority of the Christian people and the phenomenon of reception, the authority of the person and of conscience, and the teaching of the Church Fathers, doctors, and theologians.*

333. We recognize the authority of *the faith handed on by the apostles* through their living proclamation, and to which the Scriptures give a particular witness. In its diverse expressions, this tradition provided a fertile context for the composition of the books of the New Testament. This living tradition is prior to the Scriptures, for the faith of the first churches was authentic well before the writing of the New Testament books and before they were established as an authoritative body of texts.

334. This living and original tradition is not to be confused with the ensemble of post-apostolic traditions that came to enrich or modify, and sometimes even alter the life of the church. We believe that this original tradition was preserved in order to maintain the churches in fidelity to the apostolic faith. Thanks to that original tradition, today's churches are convinced of living in the faith of the apostles. It has borne the message of the Scriptures until now in the midst of the witness and commitment of faith. Referring to Saint Augustine, the Reformation recognized this tradition:

> Thus the councils would come to have the majesty that is their due; yet in the meantime Scripture would stand out in the higher place, with everything subject to its standard. In this way, we willingly embrace and reverence as holy the early councils, such as those of Nicaea, Constantinople, . . . which were concerned with refuting errors — in so far as they relate to the teachings of faith. For they contain nothing but the pure and genuine exposition of Scripture.[8]

Yet where do we find the great witnesses and places where this tradition has found expression?

335. We recognize the doctrinal authority of the *Christian people* considered as a whole. This is what the Christian tradition has called the *sense of the faithful (sensus fidelium)* or the sense of faith *(sensus fidei)*. The Second Vatican Council taught, citing Augustine, "The universal body of the faithful who have received the anointing of the holy one (see 1 Jn 2:20 and 27), cannot be mistaken in belief. It displays this particular quality through a supernatural sense of the faith in the whole people when 'from the bishops to the last of the faithful laity,' it expresses the

---

8. John Calvin, *Institutes of the Christian Religion*, Library of Christian Classics, vols. XX-XXI, ed. John T. McNeill (Philadelphia: Westminster Press, 1960), IV, IX, 8, p. 1171.

consent of all in matters of faith and morals" (*LG* 12). A declaration of the ARCIC[9] speaks of "Christian authority" in the same sense: "This is Christian authority when Christians so act and speak, men perceive the authoritative word of Christ."[10] Luther writes, "It is a spiritual priesthood common to all Christians. . . . Each Christian is instructed and taught personally by God (Isa. 54:13). According to Isaiah 11:9, 'the earth will be full of the knowledge of the Lord, as the waters cover the sea.' Thus Christ could say, according to John 6:45, 'and they shall all be taught by God.'"[11] Elsewhere, he writes, "all teachers and their teaching should and must be subject to the judgment of the listeners."[12]

336. One of the concrete ways that the Christian people exercises its authority is in the activity of *reception*. Reception is a complex phenomenon that takes place over time and can be marked by trials and tribulations. Through this process the Christian people appropriates and makes its own a teaching received from ecclesial authorities. Reception cannot be decreed in a juridical way. Whether it happens or does not, we can only be sure after it has taken place. Appropriating some teaching is more than simply accepting a spoken word; it means living it out and integrating it into the flesh and blood of the church's life. Reception is much more than simple obedience, ignorance, or refusal. It "gives meaning" to a decision, sometimes beyond what was intended by the original authors. Reception confirms that the exercise of authority was truly a service rendered to the recipients, an act ordered to their salvation. If reception is completely lacking, that means that the text bears no fruit in the church. In the former case, one can speak of the authority of the reception of a text, which is no substitute for the institutional authority which is its author, but must work together with it.

337. If the whole Christian people form a doctrinal authority, it is because *each baptized Christian* is invested with a responsibility, and thus

---

9. This is the acronym for the Anglican-Roman Catholic International Commission.

10. Anglican-Roman Catholic International Commission, "Authority in the Church I [1976]," in *The Final Report* (London: Catholic Truth Society/SPCK, 1982), no. 3, p. 53.

11. Luther, *Vom Missebrauch der Messe*, 1521, I; *WA* 8, 486-487.

12. Luther, "That a Christian Assembly or Congregation Has the Right and Power to Judge All Teaching and to Call, Appoint, and Dismiss Teachers, Established and Proven by Scripture," in *Luther's Works*, vol. 39, ed. and trans. Eric W. and Ruth C. Gritsch (Philadelphia: Fortress, 1970), p. 307.

with an authority in matters of faith. This authority is that of his or her conscience, in so far as it is inhabited by the Spirit of God. This does not mean to imply formally subjecting the content of faith to free examination.[13] It is a recognition that the act of faith can only be exercised freely and according to one's conscience. For every believer, conscience remains the ultimate instance of decision-making. The obedience of faith confers authority upon it in matters of faith. This was expressed by Irenaeus when he spoke of the spiritual disciple who judges all and is judged by no one.[14]

338. This authority of conscience is particularly demanding because it is founded in docility to the Spirit of God. It can neither be used to justify various "enthusiasms" nor can it lead to religious individualism. It is simply the place of origin for the sense of the faithful *(sensus fidelium)*.

339. Every *believer, in and through baptism,* receives the task of vigilance in doctrinal matters, according to his or her means, in particular that of judging the preaching of the gospel. This is a direct consequence of the universal priesthood of believers.[15] Obviously, the authority of each grows according to the quality of Christian living. The authority of the spiritual person, that of a martyr or mystic, and in some cases that of the poet and artist — that is to say, of those men and women whose profound spiritual experience is able to illuminate the path for others in their journey of faith — is recognized in all churches. The witness of those who are wise in the spiritual life is an authoritative point of reference.

340. Among baptized Christians, *the Fathers, doctors, and theologians* of the church exercise an authority in service of faith's authenticity. This authority may be exercised during their lifetime, yet for many of the greats among them, it continues long after their death. The authority of the early Church Fathers, who belong to the founding age of

13. The expression "free examination" is ambiguous. It can be taken in a pejorative sense, as has often been done in the Catholic Church. It can, however, be given back its correct meaning, if one understands by it a conscience that is faithful to the action of the Spirit. See above, nos. 124, 127, 132-134.

14. See *Against Heresies,* The Ante-Nicene Fathers, vol. 1, ed. A. Robins and J. Donaldson (Buffalo: Christian Literature Publishing, 1885), IV, 33, 1, pp. 506-508.

15. This more Protestant expression corresponds to the Catholic phrase, "the royal priesthood of the baptized."

the church, has a special value for it grounds the "consensus of the fathers" as a locus for theology. This reference maintains its value, even though this consensus can never be universally verified and remains but a moral consensus.

341. Every *minister* sent by the church to preach and catechize is vested with a responsibility and thus, with an authority, in the handing on of the faith. Similarly, this applies to men and women associated with their ministry ("elders," "presbyteral councilors," or "parish councilors," of the Reformed and Lutheran traditions, and lay persons in roles of responsibility or charged with an ecclesial task in the Catholic context). As well, parents and Godparents who hand on the faith to their children participate in this authority. Preaching and catechesis are contexts for the exercise of authority.

3. Institutional Forms of Authority

342. In order that these diverse authorities function in harmony and unity, there exist institutional and ministerial structures in the churches that are charged with safeguarding the communities in the unanimity of faith, while at the same time proposing a faithful living out of the gospel message. These institutions are necessary not only to avoid disorder and confusion, but even more to witness to the fact that these communities receive their faith from the message of the gospel that constitutes their ultimate authority.

343. Today the institutional forms differ from church to church and several systems are in place, in particular the episcopal system and the presbyterial-synodal system.[16] Yet all churches attribute a decisive role either to bishops, priests or pastors, doctors, councils, or synods.

16. The presbyterial-synodal system, widely adopted by churches born out of the Reformation, is a system of church governance made up of two elected collegial structures: a council directing local communities ("presbyterial") and a supra-parish structure on the regional or national level which treats questions that cannot be dealt with at the local level ("synod," functioning according to a parliamentary model). The composition of these bodies is mixed: half to two-thirds laity, half to one-third pastors or deacons. This system makes up a hierarchy of assemblies that one might call a collegial episcopate. Certain churches, especially the Lutheran churches, combine this system with a form of personal episcopate.

Before entering upon a more detailed consideration of this subject, we wish to recall together that these authorities must be exercised in keeping a threefold relationship to the communal, collegial, and personal principles. As we have already stated in our document on *The Ministry of Communion in the Universal Church*,[17] we consider this trilogy as belonging to the structure of the church.

344. *The communal dimension:* If the living gospel has been entrusted to the people of God, the exercise of doctrinal authority must take place in constant communion with the whole people, in a climate of co-responsibility and exchange. "Through this continuing process of discernment and response, in which the faith is expressed and the gospel is pastorally applied, the Holy Spirit declares the authority of the Lord Jesus Christ, and the faithful may live freely under the discipline of the gospel."[18] The people express their consent or approval in various ways, especially through the process of reception.

In the Reformation churches, the working of deliberative synods, composed variously of a third to half lay delegates, is an expression of the communal dimension. The working of consultative diocesan synods in the Catholic Church, which includes the participation of the laity, is another form for expressing this same dimension.

345. *The collegial dimension:* Ministers of the church who are responsible for ensuring the regulation of faith in the communities and for keeping them in complete fidelity to the truth of the gospel, exercise their authority in the context of a collegial collaboration, especially through synods and councils. This collaborative effort normally calls for and refers to the responsibility which is proper to the theologians who put their competency at the service of regulating the faith. Such instances of authority are always subject to the gospel according to the witness of the Scriptures. Paradoxically, this is an authority which obeys, with the very obedience of faith.

346. *The personal dimension:* Every college ought to be presided over in order to ensure that doctrinal decisions are taken effectively, conclusions drawn concerning the problems at hand, and expression given to

---

17. See Groupe des Dombes, *Le ministère de communion dans l'Église universelle* (Paris: Centurion, 1986), nos. 113-132 on the basis of the New Testament and nos. 133-162 on their expression in the Catholic Church and in Reformation churches respectively.

18. ARCIC, "Authority in the Church I," no. 6, pp. 54-55.

its unanimity. This very human fact is seen in the presiding role carried out by the apostles in the New Testament, especially by Peter,[19] no matter what consequences the churches might draw from it. The authority of a personal presider normally represents, assumes, and recapitulates that of the community and of the ministerial college.

Today, the relationship between the collegial and personal dimensions is lived out in differing ways in the Reformation churches and in the Catholic Church.

4. The Actual Working of Instances of Authority

347. A just relationship ought normally to exist between the three dimensions according to which institutional authorities have to work. A constant interaction among these three poles of authority is necessary. We note, however, that this is not always the case. Slippages are not only possible, but have existed in the past and continue to exist in our day. Certain churches have a tendency to unilaterally favor one dimension to the detriment of the other two. We shall return to this point when we come to suggestions for the conversion of the churches.

348. Whenever a new problem arises, it is normal that a period of debate accompany the reflection of the church. This is not to be feared, though it may be difficult, depending on the extent to which each believer strives to remain docile to the Holy Spirit. We see the first example of such a debate in the decision concerning circumcision taken at Jerusalem and recorded in Acts 15. When reflection on the problem has sufficiently matured, collegial and personal authorities can speak and take decisions.

349. Conflict is always possible in the life of the church, for it remains *always in need of reform (semper reformanda)* and *always in need of renewal (semper renovanda)*. The important thing is not avoiding crisis at all cost: such efforts can be self-defeating and lead to an even greater crisis. Rather, every means ought to be employed to convert the conflict into a dynamic and positive reality. If all the participants in a crisis seek to remain obedient to the gospel, the crisis can be managed in a

---

19. See Groupe des Dombes, *Le ministère de communion dans l'Église universelle*, nos. 126-128.

healthy and constructive manner. The conflicts of the past — both those which led to schism and those which brought about reconciliation — can provide us with examples of both that which is inopportune and that which builds up the church even through difficult times. A crisis ought normally to lead out of and beyond crisis.

* * *

350. A clearer picture of the major difficulties that divide us emerges from the preceding paragraphs. They do not come from the recognition of different poles of authority, for these are common to each of our churches. Rather, they are rooted in the churches' diverse manners of conceiving their actual interaction. The guarantor of a doctrinal position in the Catholic Church is the magisterium. For the Reformation churches, the criteria is the message of faith, namely, justification, with the idea that the truth will assert itself in the church and does not need a human guarantee. The functioning of synods does not follow the same logic on either side.

Section II: A Diagnosis of Remaining Divergences

351. Because our disagreements pertain to the understanding, the working out, and the interaction of diverse instances of authority, we follow the same line of development here from *texts* to *persons* and *institutional forms* in the hope of identifying that which presently divides us in the exercise of doctrinal authority.

But before proceeding further, it is appropriate to note the fundamental ideas that concern (1) our two manners of understanding the church, and (2) our two traditions of interpreting authority, which are linked to a certain understanding of redeemed humanity. These fundamental ideas lead to two concrete forms which (3) sometimes give rise to caricatured interpretations in the collective consciousness. An extended reflection from our two perspectives will allow us to better specify the implications of our divergent positions.

1. Divergence on the Church

352. The Catholic Church maintains the episcopal and thus hierarchical structure that emerged in the early post-apostolic church. This structure includes a constant exercise of doctrinal authority as a principal responsibility of the bishops in union with the pope, and in certain cases by the pope alone, yet always in communion with the church. Following the example of Orthodox Churches, the Catholic Church considers this episcopal structure as the only normal one, since it is within this framework that it understands its apostolicity and catholicity.

353. The Catholic Church has always recognized the structural role of synodality and collegiality in its doctrine. In the course of its early and modern history, it has held numerous councils and synods. Yet it is true that it has increasingly placed a value on personal authority in the person of the bishop in the local church and of the pope at the level of the universal church. The centralizing trend of the second millennium has led to the concrete form that it has today.

354. The churches born in the Reformation contested the ecclesial power in force in the medieval church. The Reformers sought to distinguish that which subsists of the "true" church of Christ, despite doctrinal and practical deviations. Their criteria were determined by the power of the Word of God actualized among believers, to whom "the gospel is purely preached and the holy sacraments are administered according to the gospel,"[20] in the "company of the faithful who agree to follow his Word and the pure religion which it teaches."[21] These criteria conferred a secondary role of service on both the church and its ministers in relation to the preeminence of the gospel, and left each local church the freedom to organize its own institutions, operations, and liturgical practices. None foresaw the development of a new ecclesiology or the establishment of another church. The concrete organization of the Reform movement was above all linked to historical and contextual factors. Thus it was that the concern for local communities took precedence as did their close connection within regional and national territories, to the

---

20. "Augsburg Confession," in *The Book of Concord: The Confessions of the Evangelical Lutheran Church*, ed. Robert Kold and Timothy J. Wengert (Minneapolis: Fortress, 2000), Art. VII, p. 42.

21. *Confession of La Rochelle*, Art. XXVII. www.creeds.net/reformed/frconf.htm.

detriment of a reflection on the universal church, a concern that was nonetheless very present in the thought of the Reformers.

355. Due to the doctrinal dispute concerning the "power" of the pope and of the bishops, and the break which usually occurred between new ecclesiastical authorities and the bishops of the Catholic Church, the Reformation churches most often adopted a presbyterial-synodal structure. This gave a prominent role to the synodal and collegial dimensions of the church. Certain Reformation churches preserved or later recovered an episcopal office.

356. The Reformation insisted on the tension between the "invisible" church (or the church "before God") and the "visible" church (or the church "before humankind"), as constitutive to the existence of the church. The former expression evokes the true church of Christ confessed in the creed, which remains essentially one in spite of human divisions. The latter speaks to the human and institutional reality with its unwieldiness, its hierarchies, its conflicts and divisions. Now the structuring of doctrinal authority and of ministry, and therefore of the institutional organization, flow from the latter and do not belong to the heart of the invisible church. They serve the Word of God; they are second (yet never secondary!). Because of this, they undergo various developments according to their geographic and historic contexts. While the "foundation" of the Church in Jesus Christ cannot be called into question by human voices, the diverse "forms" it takes are not only legitimate, but desirable, for they reveal the richness of the expression of the Christian faith. Yet this distinction between the "foundation" and the "forms" of the church must not be understood as an acceptance of division among Christians. Such a view, to the extent that it engenders divisive antagonisms, is born not from the riches of diversity, but rather from mutual rejection and exclusion.

357. The following question is often put to the Catholic Church: Is there only one form or model of the church, that of the Catholic Church? Or can these two structures — episcopal-hierarchical and presbyterial-synodal — be reconciled in full communion? What is the sacramental deficiency *(defectus)* and the defect of communion and unity that affects the Reformation churches in the eyes of the Catholic Church? Reciprocally, what is the deficiency of collegial communion and the institutional excess affecting the Catholic Church in the eyes of the Reformation churches? Just how far can this debate go?

2. Divergence on Authority Conferred
on the Person of the Believer

358. The manner in which the Catholic Church understands the human person saved by grace through faith leads it to accept with confidence that the authority of Christ is truly entrusted to persons who remain sinners. It considers that, with the help of the Holy Spirit, they can truly express the gift given to the church to remain in the truth of the apostolic faith until the end of time.

359. The Catholic Church understands doctrinal authority as one of the three "powers"[22] with which it has been entrusted, that of announcing the gospel in truth to every creature. This proclamation includes, as a necessary corollary, a certain self-regulation, in order to safeguard the authenticity of the apostolic faith as a treasured deposit. This function is carried out by the "magisterium" which ensures at the same time the proclamation of faith and its regulation through a series of texts and documents. The earliest of these in date and those which bear the most authority are the confessions of faith. They are all intended to propose and interpret the apostolic message in the context of their times and cultures, and as a function of the crises or disputes encountered by the church.

360. Different levels of the church's doctrinal authority are involved in proportion to each case at hand. Certain documents can become quickly outdated. The chosen formulation must be understood in relation to the precise intention of the various councils and popes. To simplify the complex hierarchy of the various documents, one could say that in general documents having *universal import* are considered to involve either an *indefectible* or *infallible* authority.

361. To say that a document is promulgated in an *indefectible* manner is to affirm that in proposing such a teaching the Catholic Church has not been unfaithful to the gospel or to its saving mission. In this sense, it has not "erred," because it judged, at a particular moment of history, such a teaching to be necessary in the service of the faith and of ecclesial communion. This indefectibility does not at all mean that the content professed in the document is irreformable. There are many

---

22. The three powers or three functions are those of teaching (doctrine), sanctification (sacraments), and government (jurisdiction).

cases where teachings and decrees with a universal import have fallen into disuse[23] in relation to the living doctrine of faith, or have even been set aside to make room for other decisions.

362. A document is said to have been proclaimed *infallibly* when the promulgating authority — either an ecumenical council or the pope speaking *ex cathedra* (that is, *from the chair of Saint Peter*) — manifests, without a doubt, its intention to confer on it an *irreformable* character. This applies the definition of dogma. The irreversible character pertains not to the formulation in itself, which can be continually improved, but rather to the fundamental object of the affirmation. The dogmatic formula, always perfectible, expresses an open orientation between two points on a compass, while excluding positions outside their scope.

363. Throughout history the development of diverse dogmatic definitions has built up a "doctrine of faith." Their cumulative effect has produced a corpus of doctrinal texts whose authority is presented according to a juridical formality.[24] The continuity of doctrine is emphasized, their homogenous development, rather than their evolution through the centuries. Documents of the past considered as definitive are always assumed by new texts, even though they might need to be improved upon, completed, or even corrected.

364. Of course, these documents are all subject to the unwritten law of reception, with its vicissitudes and surprises. Through the process of reception a document goes from the status of a formal authority to that of a concrete point of reference. For texts are always born in

23. The twenty-second *Dictatus papae* of Gregory VII, cited in no. 100 above, must be understood in this sense. It affirms that "the Roman Church has never erred and, according to the witness of Scripture, will never err." It is worth noting that these *Dictatus papae* are no longer included in the collection of Denzinger (see the note that follows).

24. The work initiated by H. Denzinger in 1854, *Enchiridion Symbolorum, definitionum et declarationum de rebus fidei et morum,* which recently appeared in its 38th edition, the bilingual version entitled *Symbols et definitions de la foi catholique* (Paris: Cerf, 1996), gathers the documents of the magisterium of the Catholic Church from the first confessions of faith up to more recent declarations. While these texts are official, their selection remains the work of private theologians. Critiques are taken into account from one edition to the next: certain documents are removed, others added. [For a comparable contemporary English language work, see J. Neuner and J. Dupuis, eds., *The Christian Faith in the Doctrinal Documents of the Catholic Church,* 7th rev. ed. (New York: Alba House, 2001). The latter includes a number of significant ecumenical agreed statements. — Trans.]

the living consciousness of the church as it announces and hands on its faith. The document of a regional council can be received in a universal[25] manner and thus find itself vested with a great deal of authority, while the decision of an ecumenical council can be forgotten.[26]

365. The manner in which the Reformation churches consider the human person saved by grace through faith leads them to a fundamental reservation with regard to all human instances of authority exercised in the church. These churches appeal spontaneously to Christ, to the gospel, and to the sovereign authority of the Scriptures beyond the actual exercise of authority by established structures. They always see in those who hold positions of authority a person who is at once justified and a sinner. The affirmation that the believer is indeed wholly graced by God, while remaining entirely under the grip of the "old self" in daily life, applies also to the church: fully graced in Christ, and thus inerrant and infallible in its proclamation of the gospel, the church is also truly sinful (and not only because of the sins of its members) in its human reality, its organization, and its decision-making structures. If, therefore, Reformation churches are fully confident in the divine partner of the Covenant, they judge that the human partner will always receive the gift of the Covenant in a fragile and precarious manner.

366. As we saw in our historical survey, the Protestant Reformers proposed a concept of doctrinal authority that was very different from the one held by the Catholic Church on the basis of four major points of reference, bound through the relationship between inward and outward realities.[27] A "dialectic of permanent and mutual regulation" takes place between these two levels. The community is a corrective to the risk of sliding into individualism. The believer is there to prevent

---

25. For example, the canons of the Council of Orange of 529 on the doctrine of grace.

26. For example, the condemnation of the *Three Chapters* by the Council of Constantinople II in 553, directed against Theodore of Mopsuestia, Ibas of Edessa, and Theodoret of Cyrus, whose doctrine was considered to be too "Nestorian." See above, nos. 69-75.

27. See above, no. 127f. On the inward level the sovereign authority of the Scriptures (1st reference), entrusted to the inner testimony of the Holy Spirit in the conscience of the believer (2nd reference). On the outward (or "visible") level, the public witness of the church as a "collective person of believers" (3rd reference), and the normative confessions of faith (4th reference), which always remain subject to revision or redefinition.

ecclesial authorities from "muzzling the Holy Spirit." We saw above how this dynamic equilibrium has given way to the preeminence of the individual conscience over all communal authorities resulting in a serious weakening of doctrinal unity within the Protestant churches.

367. As the Scriptures and the confessions of faith always need to be actualized in history, the Protestant tradition entrusted regulatory authority for the content of faith to the doctors of the faculties of theology inherited from the Middle Ages. On the other hand, "synods" took on the other task of authority, becoming primary communal instances for examination, decision-making, and application of doctrines. A certain creative tension remains between these two authorities, at times giving rise to conflict.

368. Whereas the Catholic understanding emerges in a continuous and linear manner, the Protestant understanding includes a fundamental dialectic of the "total" ambivalence of contraries according to the principle of *at once justified and yet a sinner (simul justus et peccator)* in the heart of doctrinal authority. This perspective applies equally to the relationship between authority and truth: inerrancy and infallibility, holiness and purity, but also contingency and historical relativity, sinfulness and fallibility, and infidelity and lack of faith characterize the exercise of doctrinal authority. The Protestant concept juxtaposes disruption to linear continuity, in the interest of a church that is *always in need of reform (semper reformanda)* by the power of the gospel, which remains its master.

3. Two Divergent and Oversimplified Images of the Church

369. It is not surprising that such different understandings of the church and its doctrinal authority contribute to very diverse concrete images expressed in a certain number of popular "clichés" which, though not entirely unfounded, can lead to a caricature of what the church is. By gathering together these contrasting images we can come to see the risks of doctrinal drift affecting our respective churches and envisage areas in need of conversion for the future.

370. Without claiming in any way that the image of the Catholic Church can be reduced to these ways of viewing it, we readily acknowledge that it appears as a great hierarchical pyramid in which the people

— the "laity" — have little place. It is perceived as a body of clergy where bishops, and above all the pope, maintain a quasi-monopoly of speech. Thus, one spoke commonly of the "teaching church" and the "learning church," expressions that one would be hard pressed to find in Scripture. Its institutional form is often considered sacred, even in the most minute detail. Signs of respect due to each representative of the hierarchy can lead to a cult of personality. Yet this classic and monolithic image is breaking down today due to the influence of the Second Vatican Council and a more critical reflection by Catholics concerning their church.

371. In its doctrinal expression, the Catholic Church also appears as a governing body constantly intervening with authority on numerous subjects, in particular in the field of ethics, where debate is reduced to a minimum. It is perceived as a body where theologians are closely monitored, where everything is decided from above by the hierarchical authority, and where one is required to follow the official position. Freedom of conscience is recognized, but is considered as a secondary and conditioned point of reference. One gets the impression that the Catholic believes whatever the magisterium tells him or her to believe, however it chooses to express the faith.

372. The Reformation churches appear as little regional entities whose autonomy gives rise to a certain doctrinal erosion. The institution is reduced to a minimum and synods function according to a democratic model where decisions are taken by majority vote. This sometimes leads to surprising debates. The large place accorded to the role of the individual conscience leads some to entertain the idea that Protestants do not feel bound by any other authority. It seems as if they never consider that a doctrinal authority can speak a definitive word. Freedom of expression in the realm of faith produces a climate of confusion which does not appear to be sufficiently balanced by the sense of community and responsibility. Reformation churches exhibit a lack of openness, interest, or sensitivity for the universal church. A major problem with this ecclesiology is the relationship between the local churches and the universal church, as is the relationship between the individual conscience and the ecclesial consensus.

373. In the realm of doctrine, the ultimate authority which binds the faith of Protestant Christians is the Word of God acknowledged by the conscience. In practice, some are led to say, "I believe what is writ-

ten in the gospel and what the Spirit teaches," or more simply, "I believe what my conscience tells me." Undoubtedly, an even greater number would say, "I believe what I can in solidarity with the community," or again, "I believe what I believe, that is, I know in whom it is that I believe." This image of faith appears to other Christians as excessively individualistic and hardly compatible with the requirements of a universal communion in one faith.

4. A Different Consideration of Texts

374. Catholics and Protestants do not have the same fundamental attitude regarding texts. This difference begins with the Scriptures themselves. Both acknowledge their "inerrancy," the fact that they convey the truth regarding the salvation of humankind, yet there are important and sometimes conflicting nuances among Protestant tendencies toward fundamentalism or liberalism. Catholics and Protestants respond differently to the question, "How am I bound by the Scriptures on such and such a question?" The appeal to Scripture in general can become a slogan, whenever its words get in the way of our cultural presuppositions.

375. Attitudes concerning biblical exegesis are closer than ever among Catholic and Protestant scholars. They take part in beneficial opportunities for exchange and close collaboration, recognizing the scientific quality of one another's research.

Nonetheless, the doctrinal attitude concerning the authority of Scripture remains the object of considerable difference. The Protestant feels bound by the fundamental doctrine of justification by faith, or sometimes even more so by the demands of his or her personal conscience before the Word of God. He or she is less concerned by theological doctrines or official decisions. The Catholic will be much more concerned to reconcile the truth uncovered by contemporary research in the human sciences and exegesis with the truth of faith, as expressed in the traditional teaching of the church. The way of thinking about the authority of the Word of God as conveyed by the discourse of church, in the diversity and contingency of writing in human words, is not the same.

376. The authority of the *confessions of faith* does not function in the

same way on each side. For Catholics, their content is an absolute and irreformable point of reference due to their apostolic origin. For Protestants, they have a more relative and subtle authority. This difference, though hardly noticeable with regard to the early creeds, becomes more pronounced with the sixteenth-century confessions. From a Catholic perspective, new confessions of faith are complementary explanations of the early creeds. While in the Lutheran churches the confessional texts of the sixteenth century remain unchanged and retain their theological normativity, they are not necessarily well known by the communities. Certain Protestant churches developed other "declarations of faith" in the twentieth century, but these texts do not enjoy the same degree of authority as the early creeds, having a contextual and limited value, given the critical situations from which they emerged.

377. While biblical exegesis has made considerable progress in its consensual manner of understanding the act of interpreting[28] a text, the same cannot be said concerning the exegesis of *ecclesial, conciliar,* or *confessional documents.* This discipline has been noticeably slow to develop, though it has been the object of important and beneficial studies. This raises a decisive question for the Reformation churches: how and where does one look to find contemporary developments in the reforming tradition? Which texts are authoritative today, and how?[29] In other words, what is the confessional identity of the heirs of the Reformation today? In this regard, two dangers lie in wait for us: relativism and literalism.

378. Relativism is a more specifically Protestant temptation. It emphasizes the cultural and historical limitations and the largely outdated character of early texts. It grants little authority to contemporary documents, which it considers to be eminently revisable. This temptation can also affect certain Catholic milieus.

379. Literalism with regard to magisterial texts is a more specifically Catholic temptation. Concern to constantly respect the irreformable statement of faith has led to maximalist interpretations of certain documents, such as those of Trent and Vatican I, and to the danger of reducing the realm of indefectibility to that of infallibility.

---

28. *Hermeneutics,* in scientific terms.

29. For example, one might consider the 1938 *Declaration of Faith* of the French Reformed Church, which is solemnly proclaimed at the beginning of every synodal assembly.

Moreover, it encourages certain tendencies of Catholic opinion to treat papal documents like an arsenal of timeless *proof texts (dicta probantia)* of equal weight that can be brandished about in defense of questionable causes.

380. Oddly enough, according to certain theses recalled above, the authority of the sixteenth-century confessional statements — in particular in the Lutheran tradition — can also give rise to literalist readings that view every reformulation and effort of doctrinal reconciliation as an unacceptable abandonment of the vigorous thought of the Reformers. We witnessed a recent example of this in the negative reactions which preceded the signing of the Lutheran-Catholic agreement on justification by faith.

5. Divergent Considerations of Communities and Persons

381. Catholics and Protestants alike recognize the authority of the individual conscience and the collective conscience of the Christian people considered as a whole. Yet we note an overemphasis on the appeal to the individual conscience among Protestants to the detriment of the regulating effect that a reference to the whole body of the Christian faithful can bring, while Catholics give preference to a vision of the authority of the people of God, whose unanimity is recognized as an infallible expression of faith. This is the doctrine of the *sense of the faithful (sensus fidelium)* recalled above, or of the *sense of faith (sensus fidei)* of all the faithful.

382. Thus, the autonomy of the believing subject and the relationship of the personal conscience to authority are not understood in the same way. On the Catholic side, the right of conscience is affirmed vigorously. In a certain way it is understood as absolute, because every will that is at variance with conscience is evil. Thomas Aquinas went so far as to say that belief in Christ, which is a good thing in and of itself, can become an evil when reason proposes it to the conscience as evil.[30] The right to religious liberty forbids all coercion of the erroneous conscience, even in the case of invincible ignorance. On a lighter note, the Catholic Newman did not hesitate to say, following the definition of

---

30. Thomas Aquinas, *Summa Theologiae*, Ia IIae, q. 19, art. 5, *in corpore.*

papal infallibility, "Certainly, if I am obliged to bring religion into an after-dinner toast (which indeed does not seem quite the thing), I shall drink — to the pope, if you please — still to conscience first, and to the pope afterwards."[31]

Nonetheless, an erroneous conscience is not a good thing. Freedom of conscience, if it is to be exercised legitimately, entails the responsibility of every person to seek the truth and to become as well informed as possible. In the case of opposition with those who have been entrusted with doctrinal authority in the church, the burden of proof is incumbent on the conscience.

383. While the Catholic Church has declared unambiguously the authority of the *sense of the faithful (sensus fidelium)*, it remains very reticent in its manner of consulting and taking account of it. According to its institutional logic, it is through the bishop, who is attentive to the faith of his people, that things are to be brought from the grassroots to the attention of the universal authority. Yet the downward movement from texts, from the pope and the bishops toward the faithful, takes priority over the movement from the authority of the faithful toward texts and the ministers in charge. On the other hand, within Protestantism where the synodal structure remains close to the local churches, reference to the consensus of the church can become a tributary of the current dominant opinion. In such a case, the synodal decision taken by a relative majority or by fifty percent of the votes plus one possesses only a relative representational character. It can generate dissension and even new divisions, rather than enabling the recovery of consensual unity.

384. Who is the doctor of faith? Who assumes the role as vigilant assessor in determining what is in conformity to the gospel? Here again responses differ. For Catholics, the exercise of the magisterium of faith is reserved to the pope and the bishops. Theologians undoubtedly have an important role in the church and render an indispensable service to the exercise of the magisterium, notably in the case of the councils. They are consulted regularly. Nonetheless, they no longer en-

---

31. John Henry Newman, "A Letter Addressed to the Duke of Norfolk on Occasion of Mr. Gladstone's Recent Expostulation [1874]," in *Certain Difficulties Felt by Anglicans in Catholic Teaching*, vol. 2 (London: Longman, Green, and Co, 1900), 5.4. www.newmanreader .org/works/anglicans/volume2/gladstone/section5.html.

joy the doctrinal authority that was recognized as belonging to faculties of theology in the Middle Ages.[32] They no longer have a deliberative vote, and instead carry out their service under the authority of the magisterium.

385. For Protestants, theologians continue to be an important reference of the poles of doctrinal authority. The Reformation has always recognized an important degree of authority in the doctors of the faculties of theology for expressing the content of faith. The authority of synods, which happens to include laity and pastors, functions as a communal regulator of the theologian's thought.

386. On the subject of episcopal ministry, the Groupe des Dombes continues to stand by the positions and proposals that it took in the document of 1976.[33] It presents the foundation of *episkopé* in the New Testament and shows that *episkopé* extends beyond the ministry of the *episkopos* alone. Nonetheless, this ministry took on the dominant figure of the personal ministry of the episkopos at the moment of transition from the apostolic to the post-apostolic church.[34] The document affirms that "episkopé brings together both collegiality and the presidency of individuals" (no. 31) and situates it within the structure of the church.[35]

Nonetheless, our group is aware of the fact that these are its own positions and that they do not constitute a universal agreement established between the churches. There continue to be numerous divergences concerning the normativity of the episcopate. Within the context of a reflection on doctrinal authority in the church, the question

---

32. See above, no. 102.

33. See *Le ministère épiscopal* (Taizé: Les presses de Taizé, 1976). [English translation: "The Episcopal Ministry: Reflections and Proposals Concerning the Ministry of Vigilance and Unity in the Particular Church," *One in Christ* 14 (1978): 267-288.]

34. "At the time when the New Testament was sketching out the ministry of *episcope,* the apostolic writings had not been defined as Scripture any more than *episcope* had been defined as a ministry. Yet it was the churches presided over by *episcopoi* who gradually received the canon of Scripture. To say this is to acknowledge that the churches which referred themselves in a definitive way to Scripture were right in considering that this was the basis of the ministry of their *episcopoi.*" See "The Episcopal Ministry," no. 23, p. 277.

35. "Faithfulness to what Christ intended consists in respecting this structure without trying to draw from the New Testament any one normative model of organization." See "The Episcopal Ministry," no. 31, p. 278.

of a collegial or personal form of episcopal ministry continues to be debated as if at a crossroads.

387. On the Catholic side, the doctrine of papal infallibility, in certain cases and under certain conditions, was defined by the First Vatican Council. In such cases the pope is enabled to express the infallibility of the whole church. This doctrine is considered irreformable in its fundamental object, yet also as perfectible in its meaning and expression. Infallibility pertains only to the domain of doctrinal statements and not to the life of the popes,[36] nor of the church. This was recognized officially in the recent acts of repentance carried out by Pope John Paul II in Rome, Jerusalem, and Eastern Europe.

388. On the Protestant side, the doctrine of papal infallibility raises many problems. The very idea seems ambiguous, since in common speech the idea of *infallibility* is associated with *impeccability*. A *fallible* person is one who can *fail*, be *a failure* at something, and also *sin*. Now it does not appear that the popes were "impeccable" men throughout history. Further, if one admits the fundamental idea of the infallibility of the church, it does not seem justifiable to lay it on the shoulders of a single person.

The idea of infallibility is also criticized because it belongs to an abstract, Latin, and juridical vocabulary, unrelated to biblical language where the theme of covenant is dominant. It is the divine partner who keeps his promise, and God's fidelity that maintains the church in its fidelity throughout the history of their relationship. Finally, the exercise of authority by the pope over the course of history has led the Catholic Church to add new explanations[37] to the Christian faith which go beyond the witness of Scripture.

6. Divergent Functioning of Institutional Authorities

389. In light of the three dimensions of ministry, the communal, collegial, and personal,[38] the Catholic Church has clearly favored the per-

---

36. The German word *unfehlbar* bears within it the idea of sinlessness as much as infallibility, for *fehlen* means to fail, to commit a fault, to sin.

37. For example, the Marian dogmas.

38. See Groupe des Dombes, *Le ministère de communion dans l'Église universelle*, nos. 133-162.

sonal dimension to the detriment of the other two. For almost a thousand years it has lived in a dynamic of increasing centralization, particularly in the realm of doctrinal authority. There is a real imbalance, though this is reflected more in practice than in doctrine.

390. It is no less clear that the churches born out of the Reformation favor the communal and collegial dimensions. Certain churches among them, having a more congregational polity, even prefer to retain the communal dimension alone. Given the recognized role of episcopal ministry in the Catholic Church and in other churches, in particular the Anglican and Orthodox churches, this imbalance also takes on a doctrinal character.

391. It follows that the activity of synods is very different. On the Catholic side, the role of synods — whether it be a triennial synod of bishops in Rome, continental synods, or diocesan synods — is strictly controlled. Not all synods meet regularly. Their convocation and composition depends upon the initiative of the bishop or the pope. They are not normally deliberative, but have only a consultative voice. Those who convoke them remain free to accept or reject their expressed wishes.

392. On the Protestant side, synods are the normal means for the exercise of doctrinal authority. They meet regularly and enjoy a fully deliberative role. However, their decisions are only binding upon the churches gathered there, a fact which makes supra-national decision-making extremely difficult. Further, the decisions taken can be challenged by the following synod, which makes it difficult to arrive at an enduring decision. Mention must also be made of the considerable importance of the representational role of persons delegated to the synod. Their mandate is often short term, which can be prejudicial to their synodal formation and awareness of the implications of the decisions to be taken.

393. On the Protestant side, synods function according to the democratic principle of majority vote, sometimes modified. Has this principle been adequately critiqued? Will the Holy Spirit always be on the side of the immediate majority? The history of the church would suggest not. On the Catholic side, according to the tradition of the early church that is greatly respected by the Orthodox churches, synodal assemblies normally seek at least a moral unanimity. Here one runs the risk of settling for a shallow compromise. Can the Holy Spirit always be found in a unanimity that can become artificial?

394. The Catholic Church also gathers in general and ecumenical councils. These councils have a fully deliberative vote, while remaining under the authority of the pope, who alone can convoke them legitimately. They also have need of his confirmation in order for their decrees to be applied in the church.

Because of the emphasis on the local church, Reformation churches have not conferred any normative authority on a general council since the Diet of Augsburg (1530). Today they gather regularly in world confessional organizations (for example, the Anglican Communion, Lutheran World Federation, World Alliance of Reformed Churches) to debate their future directions. They do not confer doctrinal or ecclesial authority on any of the organizations of the confessional families, as full power remains in the synods of the churches. Neither does their understanding of a regional or national council correspond to that of Catholic theology. The whole weight of their thought favors the superiority of an assembly over its president.

*   *   *

395. This accumulation of divergences might seem discouraging. They concern the very understanding of the church and the capacities of redeemed humanity. They are expressed in relation to every locus and form of authority that we, nonetheless, have in common. Even though the differences analyzed here are not always church-dividing, by their antinomic character they can nonetheless undermine our dialogues and slow their progress. We do not wish to avoid these questions; our backs to the wall, we prefer to face squarely what still separates us.

396. It is necessary to carry out this exposé of our differences and divergences, for ecumenical dialogue will only be constructive if it is built on an honest and lucid inventory of the facts. But what hope is there for reconciliation between Protestants and Catholics, one might ask, if such is the case on such a crucial matter as the problem of doctrinal authority in the church, one which commands all others? Does the radical nature of these divergences leave any hope of overcoming them? Must we conclude that the two ecclesial forms of history are incompatible and irreconcilable? Our ecumenical conviction compels us to maintain the hope that this obstacle is not insurmountable. There still remain many paths toward overcoming them which we have yet to explore.

Section III: Proposals Aimed at Overcoming These Difficulties

397. Catholics and Protestants have been in dialogue now for almost four decades, and have subscribed to a certain number of agreed statements on the doctrine of faith.[39] Most of these are undoubtedly the agreements of the dialogue commissions, and few have been ratified as such by the authorities of the churches. Yet this very fact is promising, for it means that the churches are able to have confidence at the level of doctrine and subscribe to texts considered as having the same value and weight — or should one say, the same authority — by their ecumenical partner and themselves. What would seem impossible in view of the theoretical differences of the respective churches has been made possible by the desire to understand and recognize one another.

398. The present situation of separation can be overcome by an effort of conversion accomplished by every church in its inner life on the one hand, and in the way each regards the other church on the other. This effort of conversion must extend to two levels: that of broadening the extent of doctrinal convergence that already exists, and that of practical behavior in the concrete functioning of authority. In what follows we shall discuss *in common* the effort required to transform, as much as possible, into complementary differences, those divergences and oppositions which are church-dividing today.

In chapter five of this document, we will address a number of proposals which have both doctrinal and practical dimensions to the Catholic Church and then to the churches of the Reformation.

---

39. They are so numerous, whether it be texts of international, national, regional, bilateral, or multilateral dialogues, that it would be impossible to list them all here. In the spirit of our study we are especially mindful of those in which Catholics and Protestants take part. Yet there are other bilateral texts such as Lutheran-Reformed, Lutheran-Anglican agreements, and tri-laterals such as Lutheran-Reformed-Anglican agreement. Consider the collection edited by A. Birmilé and J. Terme, *Accords et dialogues oecuméniques, bilateraux, multilatéreaux, français, europeens, internationaux* (Paris: Les Bergers et le Mages, 1995). This edition is published in the form of a binder with an index that can be continually updated. [English readers might consider the following series: *Growth in Agreement*, ed. Harding Meyer and Lukas Vischer (New York: Paulist/Geneva: WCC, 1984); *Growth in Agreement II*, ed. Jeffrey Gros, Hardin Meyer, and William Rusch (Grand Rapids: Eerdmans/Geneva: WCC, 2000); *Growth in Agreement III*, ed. Thomas Best, Jeffrey Gros, and Lorelei Fuchs (Grand Rapids: Eerdmans/Geneva: WCC, 2007). — Trans.]

399. The existence of divergences should not make us lose sight of the points of substantial agreement identified in the first part of this chapter, especially concerning the three dimensions of the exercise of authority: the communal, collegial, and personal. They must be reexamined in light of the convergence on the New Testament witness that we inventoried earlier, and that constitutes a normative point of reference.

400. One ought not to confuse doctrinal authority and its necessarily institutional form with the actual practice of its exercise at a given moment in time. We need to distinguish that which belongs to the very being of the church from the diverse concrete workings which are the result of historical developments, and are therefore relative and reformable, in the sense that the church is *always in need of reform (semper reformanda)*. We note that on both sides there are gaps and distortions between the doctrine professed and the practices in effect, more by omission on the Protestant side, and by excess or abnormal growth on the Catholic side.

1. Toward Reconciliation on the Church and the Effects of Salvation

401. We here propose a rapid treatment of a number of points whose implications extend far beyond the intention of the present document. They must be acknowledged to the extent that they relate to presuppositions that condition any chance for reconciliation on the exercise of doctrinal authority in the church.

402. Our understanding of the mystery of the church has not yet been completely reconciled, in particular concerning the relationship of its invisible and visible, the inward and outward aspects. In what sense is the gratuitous gift of God through Christ and in the Holy Spirit entrusted to human persons, received and communicated through their ministry? This is related to the degree of liberty bestowed upon the church: How far can it go in the interpretive developments that it associates with Scripture (doctrine, dogmas, etc.) and how much authority may it confer upon them? How far can we go in recognizing the assistance of the Spirit to persons and institutions who assume doctrinal authority in the church? We still have a long way to go as we progress in agreement on these fundamental matters.

403. Under what conditions can we recognize that the one church

of Christ subsists in a visibly instituted church? Further discussion is also needed concerning the criteria that would allow each church to recognize the one church of Christ in churches other than itself. First it is necessary to confirm whether they can affirm together that the churches founded on Christ can exist according to different "forms," "organizations," and "types." If this is the case, one must then ask to what extent the instances of doctrinal authority and their structuring are decisive for the mystery of the church, or whether they are simply a practical means for expressing the reality of the visible church. Does the Catholic manner of conceiving the magisterium belong to the truths of faith?

404. Would not a respect for the three communal, collegial, and personal dimensions of the church bring about a reconciliation on the episcopal structure of the church?[40] History has shown that this structure functioned in a variety of ways according to the times. It is compatible with different forms. It could work through diverse functioning among the churches which were divided in the sixteenth century and respect the emphases of their respective traditions. The dialogues on "The Church and Justification" are proceeding in this direction.

405. The agreed statements on justification by faith ought to have certain consequences for the exercise of authority in the church. Though its institutional functioning is always ambivalent, at once justified and sinful *(simul justus et peccator)*, can we not recognize together that a statement can be very simply true in regard to the faith? That is to say, that it constitutes a sure reference, recognized by both sides, even though it is always perfectible and oriented toward a richer and more complete understanding of the message of the gospel?

2. Toward Reconciliation on Texts

406. We still need to develop principles for a common doctrinal interpretation of texts that we recognize together as authoritative, including first, the Scriptures, then confessions of faith and the documents of the councils of the early church. More than a question of scientific

---

40. See *Le ministère de communion dans l'Église universelle;* and Faith and Order, *Baptism, Eucharist and Ministry* (Geneva: WCC, 1982).

exegesis, it is a matter of discerning with the help of exegesis that which binds us together in faith. How do we live out the believers' relationship of authority with these texts?

407. The reception of the canon of Scriptures is an act of confession on the part of the churches, analogous to the confession of faith. Has the sixteenth-century division on this question not lost its relevance in today's exegetical, historical, and doctrinal context? Would it not be possible to establish an agreement among all Christians with respect to the distinction between proto- and deuterocanonical books,[41] according to the model of the French language ecumenical translation of the Bible (*La traduction oecuménique de la bible*, or *TOB*)?

408. For documents published following the separation of the sixteenth century (confessions of faith, conciliar and creedal texts), each church must undertake an effort of discernment to distinguish in these texts that which is imprescriptible in the eyes of faith from historical, cultural, and polemical expressions that resulted from a situation of conflict. We must ask ourselves, in what and just how far we are bound by them today?[42] How much is contextual — and therefore reformable or susceptible to reformulation — and what is the meaning that ought to be retained? We claim that our partners are required to endorse these texts formally, given the climate and certain contents of their redaction. For example, Catholics could not subscribe to the Augsburg Confession any more than Protestants could accept the decrees of the Council of Trent in their entirety. A just way forward has been mapped out in the study of the mutual lifting of condemnations.[43] In our approach to these texts we must avoid all literalism, anachronism, or relativism.

---

41. Those books of the Old Testament written in Hebrew are called *protocanonical;* certain later works written in Greek are called *deuterocanonical.* Already the Jews were divided on this question, with Palestinian Jews retaining only protocanonical books in their canon, and Alexandrian Jews adding the deuterocanonical texts. The early church followed the Alexandrian canon, that of the Septuagint. In the sixteenth century Luther reverted to the Hebrew canon.

42. As an example, see Lutheran-Mennonite dialogue on the lifting of anathemas formulated in the sixteenth century against the Anabaptists, which, while relevant in the period of their promulgation, no longer apply to the contemporary partners. See *Accords et dialogues oecuméniques*, VII, 12-14.

43. Karl Lehmann and Wolfhart Pannenberg, eds., *The Condemnations of the Reformation, Do They Still Divide?* (Minneapolis: Fortress, 1990). This study pertains not only to the doctrine of justification but also to the sacraments and ministry.

409. We should be very clear concerning the manner in which we are still bound by these early documents today, given that churches have subscribed together to a new document. From now on we must avoid invoking our respective confessional statements for a polemical purpose on points where an official agreed statement, even one expressing a differentiated consensus, has been arrived at through ecumenical dialogue. Each church ought to consider the new agreed text as respecting those imprescriptible elements contained in their own confessional documents. All ought to consider ourselves bound together by the authority of this new agreed statement of faith. Each church could count these new documents among its confessional or magisterial texts. A formal agreement on this methodology strikes us as an essential condition for progress in the search for unity.

410. In the ongoing process initiated by the *Joint Declaration on the Doctrine of Justification*,[44] would it not be possible to establish a corpus of common doctrinal texts whose authority is recognized jointly, and in the future will be recognized by all? The corpus could easily include the early confessions of faith and the decisions of the first ecumenical councils. It could evolve progressively to include the documents of the official agreed statements of the churches. Already today a certain number of the already achieved results deserve such official recognition. Catholic and Protestant documents subsequent to the sixteenth century and to which the churches continue to refer, would henceforth be read in light of the agreed statements. Thus, a new corpus of doctrinal statements would begin to evolve, developed while respecting the communal, collegial, and personal dimensions of authority, and would be in the service of building up the doctrinal unity[45] to which the churches aspire.

3. Toward Reconciliation on Communities and Persons

411. We have yet to be reconciled on the question of the link between the witness of the individual conscience and the collective conscience

---

44. See below, no. 415.

45. "Doctrinal unity" does not mean "doctrinal uniformity." It pertains to those aspects of faith considered necessary for an authentic communion among the churches. See below, no. 451.

of the established community. When the Reformers placed an increased emphasis on the faith experience of the believer, they were not thinking of conscience in an individualistic sense. They had in mind the conscience of the believer before God and of the believer in the church, two aspects that are too often forgotten today. Reconciliation on this point has doctrinal repercussions, not to mention many practical consequences.

412. In the course of our discussions we have discovered a significant agreement of perspective on the status of official preaching in the church. The church is fundamentally infallible in the witness of faith. Preaching is a major, "strategic" locus for the exercise of doctrinal authority. The Fathers of the Church were preachers. Preaching is a gospel proclaimed! The believer receives the Word of God through the word of the church. In a sense, the faithful preacher says to his or her hearers *what the Lord has said (haec dicit Dominus)*. In order for this fact to be fully respected, it is to be hoped that the churches arrive at a common affirmation of the concrete conditions for the exercise of the preaching and teaching ministries.

413. With regard to the problem of infallibility, we acknowledge differences of tradition, approach, and sensibility. The Catholic Church emphasizes the purely doctrinal dimension: the infallibility of a doctrinal instance of authority guarantees the inerrancy of a statement. Reformation churches approach the issue in an existential manner: the idea of infallibility implies an idea of impeccability that cannot be attributed to the church. Yet together we agree that the sinful dimension of the church does not diminish the reality of the gift of God that maintains it in the truth. The abuse and misuse of authority do not imply that authority in itself is evil, but belong to the order of sin.

414. On the Catholic side, the question of a "re-reception" of Vatican I's definition of papal infallibility was raised long ago by Père Yves Congar, who was later named a cardinal. Now the church fully recognizes that "it sometimes happens that some dogmatic truth is first expressed incompletely (but not falsely), and at a later date, when considered in a broader context of faith or human knowledge, it receives a fuller and more perfect expression. . . . In addition, it has sometimes happened that . . . certain of these formulas gave way to new expressions which, proposed and approved by the Sacred Magisterium, pre-

sented more clearly or more completely the same meaning."[46] In light of this, has the time not come to reformulate the dogma of Vatican I, which remains a stumbling block for the Protestant and Orthodox traditions, within the framework of an ecclesiology of communion?[47]

4. Toward Reconciliation on the Functioning of Institutional Authorities

415. The *Joint Declaration* between the Lutheran World Federation and the Roman Catholic Church on *justification* can be considered as exemplary, even though it only implicates one of the churches founded in the Reformation tradition.[48] The signing of the document is a very hopeful event, since the signatories from each side are recognized authorities and leaders. We have yet to draw out all the ecclesiological implications of this event. If, on the Catholic side, the signatory represented the pope [Cardinal Edward Cassidy, president of the Pontifical Council for the Promotion of Christian Unity], and on the Lutheran side, the churches took this decision in their respective synods, which permitted their approval to be conveyed by the vice presidents and the secretary general of their Federation [Rev. Dr. Ishmael Noko], this shows that one might envisage them eventually delegating their doctrinal authority to some common instance of authority for major doctrinal decisions. In this way doctrinal dialogue would move from being a dialogue between commissions, to one of dialogue among the doctrinal authorities of the churches.

416. For Catholics, there is an urgent need to take the phenomenon of reception more fully into account doctrinally. To be sure, the process of reception has always been operative in this church and continues to function today. Yet it is not yet been considered as a theological factor

46. Congregation for the Doctrine of the Faith, "In Defense of Catholic Doctrine [*Mysterium Ecclesiae*]," *Origins* 3 (July 19, 1973): no. 5, p. 110.

47. See below, no. 476.

48. [In July 2006, several months after the original version of this text was published, the World Methodist Council, meeting in Seoul, chose to associate itself with this same agreement in faith. See "World Methodist Council and the Joint Declaration on the Doctrine of Justification," www.prounione.urbe.it/dia-int/m-rc/doc/e_m_rc_appendix.html. — Trans.]

of any great magnitude, or as having a role in the official interpretation of documents from the past.

*   *   *

417. As this chapter draws to a close, it is worth recalling its overall structure and purpose in order to understand the sense of what it is we are proposing. First, we presented the rich field of consensus that unites us, in the hope that in the future this consensus might be able to bear the weight of our differences, when the latter are sufficiently converted as to no longer be church-dividing. We have laid the foundations for what might become a *differentiated consensus*.

418. Next, we set out to state honestly all the points on which the churches diverge and which still constitute an important impasse. We did not try to soften this report by hiding the facts behind an irenic façade. For we are convinced that it is only by getting to the bottom of our difficulties that we can hope to one day overcome them. We further insisted on the fact that divergence most often occurs in the heart of consensus.

419. Finally, we identified several doctrinal ways forward, undoubtedly modest, with a view toward reconciliation. If there are strong divergences, our consensus is equally strong. We were borne up in this task by the historical and biblical analyses which opened new horizons for mutual questioning. While we do not claim to have resolved everything, we feel we have nonetheless demonstrated that a new doctrinal openness can serve to open up a broad program of work for present and future ecumenical dialogue. It is our hope that our churches' authorities will commit themselves to a twofold task: first, to the task of common research; following that, to agreements between churches.

420. We believe, in particular, that if each church were to recognize doctrinally the communal, collegial, and personal dimensions of the functioning of authority and to put them into practice in an intentional manner, we could move beyond the impression that is too often given of standing before two fundamentally divergent and incompatible conceptions of the church. On both sides we need to recognize and honor the distinction between that which belongs to the *essence* — or, to use another vocabulary, to the *one structure* — of the church, and all that

belongs largely to the world of *organizations* and *institutions*. Here as well, unity and communion are not uniformity.

421. We have formulated several proposals for overcoming the difficulties identified in this chapter. We shall extend this development in the next chapter by formulating diverse proposals for the conversion of the churches. Without a doubt, doctrine and practice go hand in hand in this matter, even while maintaining their specificity. Despite the church-dividing differences that have yet to be overcome, the doctrinal consensus that we have achieved until now can lead us to act in ways that will better integrate the insights of our partners into our own practices. In addition, a common way of respecting, living out, and administering doctrinal authority in the church will help us to view that which we still consider as church-dividing with eyes that are more conciliatory and renewing.

CHAPTER FIVE

For the Conversion of the Churches

422. In this final step of our document, we shall identify a certain number of proposals for the conversion of the churches in light of the teaching of Scripture and on the basis of the ways forward suggested by the previous doctrinal reflections, trying to be as concrete as possible. By advancing together in the way of ever greater collaboration, and as mindful as possible of our partners, we will undoubtedly progress and one day discover the way toward a more complete doctrinal unity. Our ways of acting inevitably influence our ways of thinking. Our fundamental differences on the church and on the capacities of redeemed humanity could then be seen in a new light. We shall therefore indicate the points on which authority might be understood and exercised more correctly, in a way that is more transparent and coherent with the faith handed down to us.

423. The distance between what we already recognize together on the topic of doctrinal authority and that to which we are called in view of ecclesial reconciliation leaves much room for the conversion of the churches. As we have said, the authority exercised in the church is not simply a human affair, but is a gift received from Christ. This gift calls us to offer a better witness to the unity of the church, to its holiness, catholicity, and apostolicity; that is to say, the requirements of the four "notes" or "marks" which belong to its foundation remain both a gift and a task. The church is "already" holy through the gift received from God to the extent that this call to holiness becomes its vocation and reason for being. The church is "not yet" holy, because its holiness is not fully within its reach and has not been fully attained. The condi-

tion of the Christian in the church — a justified sinner — belongs to this perspective of the "already" and the "not yet."

424. Authority comes from God. Its mission is to watch over unity. It serves the sanctification of believers and the holiness of the whole church. Authority, whose goal is to safeguard the catholicity of the church, combines with communion in the concern to uphold the creative tension between the demands of communion and legitimate diversity. It could never be simply a universal governance. Finally, authority belongs to the apostolicity of the church, an apostolicity which grounds it in the gratuitous plan of God and gives it a missionary character.[1] All of this is at issue in the exercise of authority in the church and motivates our call to conversion.

425. We ought to distinguish carefully between *reform* and *conversion*. The reform of the church includes its theology, institutions, and ways of acting. It implies decision-making that brings about change. But it is unlikely to succeed unless it is supported by the consensus of the Christian people, who are persuaded of the need to accept such changes in order to witness more faithfully to the gospel. Since the publication of Père Congar's *Vraie et fausse réforme dans l'Église*,[2] and especially since Vatican II, the Catholic Church has fully recognized the need for a continual reform of its institutions.[3]

Conversion is a spiritual attitude, a dynamic that we have already described at length.[4] It is a requirement that flows from the holiness of the church. In a way, it is the inner face and precondition of every reform. Since it is shared by every member of the Christian people, it is a dynamic of emulation between the faithful and leaders purifying the deformed face of our communities. It is our hope that the diverse proposals for conversion set out here might be concretized in institutional reforms.

---

1. "For the church to be 'missionary,' is to say to other generations, to different cultures, and to new human ambitions, 'I need you' — not as a property owner speaking about the neighboring field, but as a lover." M. de Certeau, "Autorités chrétiennes," *Études* (octobre 2000): 378-379. First published in *Études* (février 1970).

2. Yves M.-J. Congar, *Vraie et fausse réforme dans l'Église* (Paris: Cerf, 1950, 1968).

3. The theme of ecclesial reform is present in Vatican II's *Decree on Ecumenism* art. 6, and in the first encyclical of Paul VI, *Ecclesiam suam*, 1964.

4. See Groupe des Dombes, *Pour la conversion des Églises. Identité et changement dans la dynamique de communion* (Paris: Centurion, 1991). [English translation: *For the Conversion of the Churches*, trans. J. Grieg (Geneva: WCC, 1993).]

426. Nonetheless, conversion cannot be brought about by decree. Conversion includes an unexpected element that distinguishes it from a deliberate, voluntary act. It is more than a simple change, even if it implies a development of ideas and can lead to a reform in the life of the church. One can prepare for conversion. Such preparation requires that the churches endeavor to acknowledge their failures, their imperfections, and resistances to their calling at every level. Every call to conversion is in keeping with this perspective of hopeful waiting for the "moment of grace" when it will bear fruit through the power of the Spirit.

427. The churches must weigh the conversions to which they will have to consent from the perspective of both understanding and exercise of authority if they are to recover the bonds of unity and communion. The calls expressed in the Groupe des Dombes' statement *For the Conversion of the Churches* regarding these questions retain their force today. They have repercussions not only for our fidelity to the gospel and to tradition. It is also a question of the credibility of the proclamation of salvation entrusted to Christians, and for which they ought to have no ambition other than to remain at the school of their Master who, on the eve of his passion washed the feet of his disciples and said, "I have set you an example" (John 13:15). A conversion of authority can only be a conversion to the service of the Lord himself, brought about through the creative, sustaining, and directive activity of the Spirit.

428. We write in full awareness of our divergent views on the church outlined above. Yet we will not proceed, as we have in past, by addressing the Catholic Church and the Reformation churches separately. We will set down a certain number of concrete points on which we hold a common conviction, and from which we will attempt to draw certain consequences and make an appeal to the different churches. This will allow us to bring together our appeals: some pertain to the church to which we all belong; others are addressed to the churches of our brothers and sisters.

429. A common thread refers us back to what was stated previously concerning texts, communities, and persons, concerning the need for a free movement among the different instances of authority, and on the communal, collegial, and personal dimensions. While we inevitably touch upon the question of ministries, we do not intend to repeat what we have already stated elsewhere, wishing to concentrate instead on the administration of different types of authority.

Section I: Concerning Texts

1. Our Relationship to Scripture

430. We are in complete agreement in considering that *the exercise of authority in the church must be founded above all on the authority and witness of Scripture*. The primacy of the Bible's authority represents the heart of the Reformation. In the Catholic Church, the priority of the authority of Scripture was reaffirmed at Vatican II: "The church has kept and keeps the Scriptures, together with tradition, as the supreme rule of its faith, since the Bible, being inspired by God and committed to writing once for all, communicates the word of God in an unalterable form" (*DV* 21). Similarly, "the study of the 'sacred page' ought to be the very soul of theology" (*DV* 24).

431. Indeed, the very authority of Jesus, received and handed down through the apostles, was set down as a norm of faith in the canon of Scripture as the passing of time distanced new generations from the first witnesses. The successors of the apostles needed an authority to refer to.

432. Scripture continually poses the challenge of interpretation. The exercise of authority in this regard is always an authority of obedience to its message. It is a *witness of faith in the service of communion* to which all Christians are called. Together we confess that Scripture must always be interpreted under the witness of and with the assistance of the Spirit. We recognize that its interpretation inevitably involves human mediations carried out in the church.

433. Vatican II clarified and restored the balance between Scripture, tradition, and magisterium in a decisive manner. For this reason, we look for the Catholic Church and its magisterium, which bears official responsibility for the interpretation of Scripture, to demonstrate more clearly how its doctrinal decisions are guided by Scripture and are obedient to its witness. To achieve this, they might take greater care to appeal to the episcopal college, to the proven results of biblical exegesis, and to the *sensus fidelium*. We request that they take the greatest care to take into account the results of ecumenical dialogue in their language and in taking positions on matters of doctrine.

434. The Reformers defended a concept of authority based on the twofold mediation of Scripture and the Holy Spirit in the face of a hier-

archical and monarchical model which they judged unfounded in the categories of the gospel. The principle of Scripture alone *(sola scriptura)* could not be legitimate in practice without an appeal to the witness of the Spirit.[5]

We look for the Reformation churches to reflect more fully in practice the value of the ecclesial dimension of this interpretation, especially when new problems arise. They must know how to take clear positions on points where they are bound by the Scriptures, and do so authoritatively. *Sola scriptura* should not be understood as a kind of individualism before God. This also implies a clarification of the relationship between the recognized authority of synods and the recognized authority of theologians. A new attitude is essential from the perspective of both their own faithful and other churches. This effort should be accompanied by a concern to collaborate as much as possible and to take account of theological convergence with other churches.

435. In the interpretation of Scripture, Reformation churches are invited today to convert their perspective and consider the authority of the ecclesial past prior to the sixteenth century as belonging fully to their spiritual patrimony. In doing so, they would be following the Reformers who referred readily to the Fathers of the Church. But the schism of that age led the churches to forget, to a large extent, their rootedness in the great tradition of the church. Their insistence on the principle of "Scripture alone" and the development of their own history led them to underestimate the heritage of the centuries preceding the Reformation as an indispensable reference for faith and theology. Despite the fact that aspects of the ecclesiological order were wrongly emphasized by the institutional authorities of the medieval church, we ask Reformation churches to recognize the authority of tradition, not as another source alongside Scripture, but as an irreplaceable and rich source for the handing on of Scripture and its message.

5. "Let this point therefore stand: that those whom the Holy Spirit has inwardly taught truly rest upon Scripture, and that the Scripture is indeed self-authenticated; hence, it is not right to subject it to proof and reasoning. And the certainty it deserves with us, it attains by the testimony of the Spirit. For even if it wins reverence for itself by its own majesty, it seriously affects us only when it is sealed upon our hearts through the Spirit." John Calvin, *Institutes of the Christian Religion,* Library of Christian Classics, vols. XX-XXI, ed. John T. McNeill (Philadelphia: Westminster Press, 1960), I, VII, 5, p. 80.

436. The witness of Scripture also represents an example and a requirement for the way of exercising authority in a climate of holiness and where there is a complete harmony of speaking and acting. Jesus was recognized as "the Holy One of God"[6] because of the twofold authority recognized by the crowd: the authority of his teaching and the authority by which he liberated from sickness and evil. His authoritative word was accompanied by actions that "verified" it. It was always proffered in the context of relationship. The manner in which Jesus exercised authority is to be the norm for the churches.

We ask all churches to be vigilant that the proclamation of the gospel founded in Scripture take place in this same climate, in particular, that it reflect harmony between what they profess and what they practice. A return to what characterizes such authority calls for a reexamination of the ways in which is exercised, so the gospel will be heard in truth by our contemporaries.

2. Confessions of Faith, Councils, and Other Documents: The Hierarchy of Texts

437. Together we receive the confessions of faith and doctrinal decisions of the early church's ecumenical councils. We concur in recognizing the necessity of formulating a communal expression of faith. Since the beginning of our separation, each of our churches has expressed the faith of the church in confessional, creedal, conciliar, or other texts. There is a hierarchy in the authority of these different documents. Today our churches officially subscribe to new doctrinal agreements. All these documents raise problems of interpretation and in this connection both literalism and relativism are to be avoided.

438. We look for the Catholic Church to clarify, without overvaluing them, the different levels of doctrinal and disciplinary authority enjoyed by the texts of the Roman magisterium and the different levels of assent that they require on the part of the faithful. We ask that it strive to present more clearly the distinction between teachings which are irreformable and those which are reformable. We ask that it put the

6. By Simon Peter (John 6:69) and also by an unclean spirit who knew and recognized him (see Mark 1:21-28; Luke 4:31-37).

principle of the "hierarchy of truths" into practice within the corpus of the faith,[7] and better integrate the notion of reception which already demonstrates a conversion to internal dialogue. We ask that it ensure that that these documents, now readily disseminated through the media, be written in a pastoral and accessible tone addressing not only the faithful, but all of our contemporaries.

Finally, we ask that it promote a correct interpretation *(hermeneutic)* of early texts, in particular the necessary distinction between the intended meaning (possibly irreformable) and the materiality of words (which can always be improved upon). The christological agreements already achieved with the Oriental Orthodox Churches establish a happy precedent in this direction.[8] We hope that a similar process, initiated by the *Joint Declaration on the Doctrine of Justification,* might be undertaken with the churches of the Reformation in regard to the treatises of the councils of Trent and Vatican I.

439. We look for the churches of the Reformation to clarify the authority recognized today as belonging to the early confessions of faith and specific confessional texts (Augsburg Confession, Confession of La Rochelle, etc.) and the criteria that ground the different degrees of authority among them. We ask them to consider whether certain conclusions of contemporary exegesis have not, in some cases, a tendency to supplant the importance of the confessions of faith. We ask that in the interpretation of their confessional texts, a greater effort be made to take into account their historically conditioned character and the need for their actualization in the present. More generally, out of concern for the communion within each and among the churches, we ask them to recognize in the institutional instances for the regulation of faith (in particular, synods, and also ecclesiastical inspectors and presidents of regional and synodal councils) all the authority they need to accom-

---

7. The organization and hierarchical ordering of the said corpus depends not on some sort of doctrinal truth that would be more fundamental than the others, but on the *relationship of each doctrinal element to the very foundation of the faith:* the saving plan of God the Father, Son, and Spirit.

8. A series of official agreements on Christology have been signed by popes Paul VI (1963-1978) and John Paul II (1978-2005) and the respective authorities of the Oriental Orthodox Churches. They established a doctrinal agreement on the meaning of the confession of faith in Christ without imposing the debated terms of Chalcedon (especially the term *in two natures*) on the partners.

pany the faithful in their fidelity to the gospel and to the faith of the church.[9]

440. We ask our churches to state clearly the extent to which they can recognize their faith in the various documents of the dialogue commissions they have mandated. In so doing, they would contribute to the reception of and progress of agreement.

We also ask them to clarify the authority accorded to the ecumenical documents that they have already signed. These documents should be included henceforth in the magisterial corpus of the Catholic Church and that of the churches of the Reformation. In making this request, we are encouraged by the promising examples of the confessions of christological faith signed between the Catholic Church and the Oriental Orthodox Churches, and of the *Joint Declaration on the Doctrine of Justification* between the Catholic Church and the Lutheran Churches. In documents such as these we see the first signs of an authority exercised jointly by the Catholic Church and by other churches. *They allow us to hope for a day where we will assume the ministry of doctrinal authority with one voice,* in humble faithfulness to the Word of God and in patient listening to what the Spirit is saying to the churches.

Section II: Concerning Communities

441. The following requests are in keeping with the framework of an ecclesiology of communion. They are directed toward respect for the person of every believer and the necessity for everyone to recognize the urgent requirement to live a common and fraternal faith not only in base communities or parishes, local and regional churches, but also within the communion that must gather all the churches. They also reflect a concern that every member of the faithful might participate responsibly, in the name of their baptismal authority, in the reflection and teaching that the churches undertake in every age.

---

9. The conduct of certain Protestant traditions of a more fundamentalist nature poses a challenge for the churches of the Reformation due to an understanding of *sola scriptura* that leaves little place for institutional regulation.

1. The Authority of Conscience

442. Together we recognize the authority of the personal conscience as the ultimate instance for all human decision-making. When we speak of conscience, we mean a responsible conscience that does everything it can to form a judgment, a Christian conscience that strives to listen to the Spirit. Only the inner witness of the Holy Spirit can guarantee that a doctrinal expression of the Word of God correctly interprets a divine truth. We saw with Irenaeus the considerable role played by a spiritual rereading of Scripture in the early church, that is to say, by the "spiritual disciple's" meditation and interpretation. This reading is perfectly compatible with the rule of faith. Yet our ways of referring to conscience differ greatly.

443. We look for the Catholic Church to be more attentive in its teaching to the conscience and experience of believers in the various domains of faith and morals, and to trust in the action of the Spirit in their hearts. This reference, though clearly expressed in the works of the most widely recognized theologians (such as Thomas Aquinas), often remains implicit. We think that the complex relationship which exists between the authority of conscience and the authority of the magisterium deserves to be made explicit. We also ask that the weight of the collective conscience of Catholics be better taken into account when it is shared in an enduring way through space and time, even if it cannot claim to represent the universal sense of faith belonging to all the faithful.

444. We look for the churches of the Reformation to underscore the Christian requirements of a correct exercise of the rights of conscience and to clarify the widespread misunderstandings surrounding the expression "free examination" that exaggerate the notion of spiritual independence and individual religious experience. A legitimate "free examination" can only be exercised thanks to the action of the Spirit and cannot cast aside the community's expression of faith. It must be exercised with the "sense of the church," of a church which reaches beyond the local context and the context of out time.[10] The

10. At the Diet of Worms (1521), Luther replied to the authorities of the established church and of the empire that it was "dangerous to go against one's conscience." He appealed to the gospel and to the council against the demands of the Roman authorities in his case.

Protestant churches are called to a conversion regarding what has, at times, been a lack of fidelity to the sense of the church and its four "marks." This will require a reconsideration of the general problem of the church's authority in relation to obedience to Jesus Christ, and re-situating the individual conscience in the context of the sense of the church.

445. Contrary to the generally accepted idea, the sixteenth-century Reformers never used the ambiguous expression "free examination." The distinction between "religions of authority" and "religions of the Spirit"[11] is only relevant on the condition that the presence of the Spirit not be reduced to a simple reflection of the human soul manifested in the spiritual experience of the individual. What has sometimes been called "Protestant spiritualism" consists, in fact, in dividing the Spirit from the church: "One thus imagines the Spirit as opposed more or less, by its very nature, to anything that resembles the 'churches.' . . . The church is continually suspected of being the enemy of individual freedom."[12] Such spiritualism, in the negative sense of the word, can lead one to claim the authority of the Spirit for the principle of individual freedom alone, in opposition to the authority of institutions, in particular, that of the church.

2. The Sense of Faith of the Faithful, Debate, and Co-responsibility

446. Christian authority also belongs to every Christian by virtue of their baptism and their participation in the common or universal priesthood. It belongs to the whole of the people of God inhabited by the "sense of faith." We know how difficult it is to accord a just place in the concrete life of the churches to this form of the authority of the individual believer and of the community and to practice a real co-responsibility between them and the established authorities. On this point, the functioning of the Catholic Church often falls short, while that of the churches of the Reformation is excessive.

---

11. See A. Sabatier, *Les religions de l'antiquité et la religion de l'esprit* (Paris: Librairie Fischbacher, 1899, 1904); new edition (Paris: Berger-Levrault, 1956).

12. Regin Prenter, *Le Saint-Esprit et le renouveau de l'Église* (Paris/Neuchâtel: Delachaux & Niestlé, 1949), p. 6.

447. Our culture accords a considerable role to *consultation* and *debate*. To be just, decisions must mature through this process. The churches cannot adopt every form of democratic debate. Nonetheless, history teaches that the functioning of church authority never occurs without a relative cultural osmosis with the ways of doing things in the course of the different periods of history.

448. We look for the Catholic Church to put the principle of co-responsibility to work as much as possible out of respect for the dignity of the laity — men and women — who are real partners of the gospel, and for the responsibility entrusted to those men and women invested with various ministries.

We especially ask that when a new problem arises in the order of faith or of morals, it leave the necessary time for debate among the local churches before taking a final decision. Let this debate be accompanied by the dialogues with other churches. Such debate ought to identify progressively the elements at play, allow the initial emotional reactions to settle, and arrive more easily at a certain consensus that will benefit the implementation of a just decision.

449. We look for the churches of the Reformation, more familiar with the culture of debate, to be vigilant that respect for differences not eliminate the necessity for a common ecclesial position rooted in the witness of Scripture. Their decision-making procedures ought to allow a frank discussion regarding the opinions of the moment and the fundamental repercussions of the faith, while being attentive to the positions of the other churches. Debate ought to be accompanied by dialogues with other churches. It ought not to drag on without taking a clear, and when needed, courageous decision. Is the Word not to be proclaimed "whether the time is favorable or unfavorable" (2 Tim. 4:2)?

450. We ask that all churches agree to share in the debate regarding problems of faith and morals which are raised in a new way, acting together to take decisions in common whenever possible, and accepting the gospel principle of mutual correction. Such collaboration, on the basis of mutual trust, will enable each church to examine itself in light of other traditions and to explain the reasons that can result in different positions.

3. Unity Does Not Mean Uniformity

451. The term *unity,* long the prime mover of the ecumenical movement with reference to the priestly prayer of Jesus (John 17), is today the object of suspicion: Doesn't it mean the wish to lead the churches to a kind of uniformity? The term *communion* is often used in preference to *unity.* While perfectly legitimate, it does not capture certain important notes contained in the latter. The position of the Groupe on this matter has always been clear. We seek the authentic unity of a reconciled church which fully respects all legitimate diversities.[13]

452. The renewal of ecclesiology and a serious ecumenical companionship has led us to appreciate just how much diversity can be of value within the context of unity. The declarations signed between the Oriental Orthodox Churches and the Catholic Church on Christology, as well as the *Joint Declaration on the Doctrine of Justification,* have put into practice a method called *differentiated consensus.* This kind of consensus on the basic imprescriptible truths of faith tolerates differences not only in the doctrinal expression of faith, but also in the emphasis on belief within the confession of the same saving mystery. In the case of the Lutheran-Catholic *Joint Declaration,* it points to doctrinal agreement on the understanding of the unity of the church beyond the mutual agreement on the understanding of salvation that was signed. In a similar way, do the churches not need to put into place a process that would be analogous to the establishment of the canon of Scripture, which remains a model of unity in diversity?

453. We look for the Catholic Church to demonstrate how, in both teaching and practice, doctrinal authority can be exercised in the service of a unity that forsakes all uniformity. Undoubtedly, the secularizing force of a century of centralization has led it to universally impose, in the name of faith, modes of thought, language, and liturgical use that at times were little more than the expression of dominant cultural particularities. Yet Paul, writing to the Corinthians, insisted in the same breath on the diversity of "charisms" and on the communion of faith. Vatican II taught an ecclesiology of communion and declared that the Catholic Church exists "in and from these particular

---

13. Our views on this point are found in the document *For the Conversion of the Churches,* concerning confessional identities.

churches" (*LG* 23). Today more than ever, unity must be achieved in accordance with the diversity of cultural situations and a legitimate pluralism of ecclesial experience.

Indeed, authority must encourage the flourishing of forms of life, spiritualities, liturgies, and theologies that, while rooted in an original way in diverse cultures, nonetheless reflect their faithfulness to the Christian faith and participation in the universal church.

454. We look for churches of the Reformation, which have often developed under the particularities of national or regional administrations, to live better the requirements of genuine church unity. Their conversion not only to an awareness, but also to a culture of unity and communion in the universal church, remains to be seen. In the wonderful expression, "differentiated consensus," the adjective should not be taken to dominate over the substantive, nor should an oversensitive respect of confessional identities prevent the renunciations necessary for the restoration of the visible unity of the church.

Section III: Concerning Collegial Authorities

455. Together we recognize the communal, collegial, and personal dimensions of authority in the life of our churches. Yet we acknowledge that the Catholic Church has trouble with the actual implementation of effective synodal institutions, for it lacks a certain culture of synodality. We note that the churches of the Reformation have a problem in recognizing the role of personal authorities capable of working within colleges and synods.

456. The churches of the Reformation are very attached to the workings of the presbyterial-synodal system. The synod, which gathers at least once a year,[14] is the supreme instrument of doctrinal authority. With the Second Vatican Council, the Catholic Church rediscovered the institution of the triennial synod of bishops in Rome. It has developed the gathering of bishops in continental synods, and introduced the new possibility of diocesan synods with the participation of the laity into its code of canon law. Nonetheless, we note that the real authority for decision-making by these synodal institutions differs greatly on each side.

---

14. According to the composition described in no. 343, note 16, above.

457. We request that the authorities of the Catholic Church not consider the gathering of diocesan synods as an exceptional event, but that they be established as an instrument that meets regularly. By so doing, they would promote the involvement of the faithful, their participation in ecclesial responsibilities, and the development of a synodal culture in the local churches. Their frequency will help to develop a mature awareness of the complexity of certain issues, and will help to steer clear of excesses. As for the hierarchy, they would be supportive of the necessary balance in the life of the church between the movement "from the top down" or from the authorities to the people of God, and the movement "from the bottom up" or from the people of God to the authorities. They must be open to receiving a relevant response to the questions they ask.

458. We ask the authorities of the Catholic Church not to fear the responsible working of the episcopal conferences, which correspond in large part to the gatherings of regional synods in the early church, and that it recognize fully their doctrinal authority, which is always exercised in communion with the see of Rome. They are genuine agents of communion not only among the dioceses of a single country or region but also within the universality of the Catholic Church. Indeed, they are a forum for regulation and discernment, responsible for the originality of cultural expressions of faith and for the recognition of legitimate diversities.

459. We request that the Catholic Church revise the rules for the triennial synod of bishops,[15] which have become so rigid that they no longer permit genuine debate, nor the progressive discernment of the clear orientation of its members on the subjects under consideration. At the same time, the method of a meeting in two parts seems unproductive.[16] It would be desirable that synods take the time necessary for a real exchange among bishops and for the drafting of a synodal text, as was the case in the first years of this institution. We would also hope that, in matters of greater importance, a deliberative authority be conferred upon the synod. These synods are an extension of the conciliar institution to the church of Rome and a strong expression of collegiality.

---

15. And, in the same vein, those of the continental synods.

16. A first period where each bishop speaks, and a period of work in small groups, following which the speeches are taken up again in a synthetic way in the form of propositions, without any real debate in the assembly.

460. We would not be so presumptuous as to call for a council! Yet we readily make our own the wishes expressed by several cardinals, in particular, Cardinal Martini, during the 1999 European Synod of Bishops, concerning "the usefulness and practical necessity for an authoritative collegial exchange of views among all bishops on certain crucial points that have come up in the course of these forty years." He therefore suggested:

> Repeating from time to time, in the course of the coming century, the experience of a universal meeting and exchange of views among the bishops, that would enable us to untie certain disciplinary and doctrinal "knots" . . . that reappear periodically as hot points in the path of the European churches, and not only of the European ones.[17]

Among the points retained by the cardinal, he includes

> the situation of women in society and in the church, the participation of the laity in certain ministerial responsibilities, sexuality, the discipline concerning marriage, penitential practice, relations with the Orthodox sister churches and more generally the need to revive ecumenical hope.[18]

461. The question of institutional instances for the expression of doctrinal authority is crucial within Protestantism. The presbyterial-synodal system comes up against a process of reception that is burdened by a scrupulous respect for each ecclesial reality. The threefold relationship of the communal, collegial, and personal is an issue within the Protestant tradition and is in serious need of balance. Ordained ministers have a preponderant role to play in this regard.

462. We ask the churches of the Reformation to conduct their synods with a greater respect for the tradition of faith and the catholicity of the church whenever they make doctrinal decisions. The bond between parishes and the church to which they belong needs to be strengthened, as does the bond to churches in other countries. For the autocephalous character of each church runs the risk of promoting an

---

17. *Documentation Catholique* 2213/3 (1999): 950.
18. *Documentation Catholique* 2213/3 (1999): 951.

ecclesial self-sufficiency due to socio-cultural and national particularities and even more to passing currents of opinion. The application of synodal decisions by parishes is important for the productive functioning of synods. Further, we would ask these churches to have the courage to confer a doctrinal authority on their world confessional organizations that would be recognized by each church; that they be more attentive to the representational role of delegates, in order to avoid the fragility of synodal decisions; and that they clarify the authority of the synod over parishes in relation to the authority of ordained or consecrated ministers and the laity.

463. We therefore request that the churches of the Reformation develop new processes for decision-making beyond the regional and national levels, and within world confessional bodies. We encourage the development of "ecclesial communions" of those Protestant churches which are already reunited, a sign that churches that were once divided can grow toward one another with Christ at their center. It is important for the witness of the churches to the gospel in the world that they visibly manifest their doctrinal communion and take decisions together on as many points as possible.

Section IV: Concerning Persons

464. We recognize the necessity for an authority exercised by persons in the life of the church. Yet agreement on this principle, more than any other, comes up against broad differences with regard to both the ecclesiological foundation and the practical functioning of this type of authority. We do not share a common culture concerning the theological and ecclesiological motives for a personalized authority. For that reason, we hope that determined and concerted efforts might bring our ways of acting closer together and enable us to explore new possibilities for a more complete communion in the future.

1. The Authority of Ministers

465. We ask that the Catholic Church make a greater effort to practice in its own daily functioning the principle of *subsidiarity*, which it has re-

flected upon at length and taught in its social teaching.[19] This principle consists in not taking from individuals the tasks which they are able to undertake on their own, and in avoiding the transfer to a higher authority of functions that those authorities more immediately concerned can normally assume. In this spirit, we would hope that doctrinal problems and conflicts might be dealt with initially at the local level or diocesan level. If the case extends beyond the diocesan boundaries, that should be dealt with by the episcopal conference and not be referred to Rome unless the conference is unable to find a solution within a reasonable time frame.

466. We ask the churches of the Reformation to reconsider the real mistrust that Protestantism bears toward all personal forms of authority. On the whole, they recognize the ministry of an ecclesiastical inspector or of a president of a regional council, and some have maintained the office of bishop. These ministries constitute an *episkopé* in connection with the synod. But the authoritative status of this personal ministry is not sufficiently known, something which has occasioned a certain number of misunderstandings within and among the churches. A better recognized ministry of presiding over a church council would be a decisive advance on the road to unity. Here again, our desire would be to arrive at a differentiated consensus. A noticeable progress in this area would benefit a better relationship among the three dimensions of authority.

467. We request that the churches of the Reformation recognize those persons who are effectively at the service of the institutional mediation for the interpretation of Scripture. Over the course of history the "Fathers" (Luther, Calvin, etc.) were vested with such authority. In doctrinal matters, the authority of the doctors and pastors is clearly recognized in principle and commended to the attention of the whole church. It is even considered as the primary purpose of their ministry. Pastors and doctors (or teachers) must hold together in their ministry the freedom of conscience and the ecclesiality of the community.[20]

---

19. See Pius XI, "*Quadragessimo anno:* After Forty Years [1931]," in *Catholic Social Thought: The Documentary History,* ed. David J. O'Brien and Thomas A. Shannon (Maryknoll: Orbis, 1992), pp. 42-79; and John Paul II, "*Centesimus annus:* On the Hundredth Anniversary of *Rerum Novarum* [1991]," in *Catholic Social Thought,* no. 48, 476.

20. In his *Institutes of the Christian Religion,* Calvin evokes this idea in terms of ecclesiastical power: "Here, then, is the sovereign power with which the pastors of the church,

2. The Doctrinal Authority of the Ministry of Unity and of Communion

468. In our document, *Le ministère de communion dans l'Église universelle,* we treated at considerable length the Catholic Church's recognition of the authority of the bishop of Rome. Yet that study did not examine his doctrinal magisterium, nor the question of papal infallibility, a point of serious disagreement among the churches.[21] We are aware of the dispute that persists on this topic for both historical and doctrinal reasons. Recent popes have acknowledged it themselves. John Paul II expressed it this way in his 1995 encyclical, *On Commitment to Ecumenism (Ut Unum Sint):* "I am convinced that I have a particular responsibility in this regard, above all in acknowledging the ecumenical aspirations of the majority of the Christian Communities and in heeding the request made of me to find a way of exercising the primacy which, while in no way renouncing what is essential to its mission, is nonetheless open to a new situation."[22] He distinguishes between the fundamental *mission* of the petrine ministry of unity and the various modalities for its *exercise.* A similar distinction is eminently applicable to the doctrinal magisterium of the bishop of Rome. This hopeful line of thought compels us to express several hopes and suggestions.

469. From the perspective of the churches of the Reformation, there are those today who readily imagine a place in the life of the church for an office that would symbolize visible unity and the communion of all the churches, presiding over, though not governing them. Though convinced that they remain faithful to the teaching of the apostles, these churches have not always known how to concretize their apostolicity — in the sense of making it visible — in the everyday

---

by whatever name they be called, ought to be endowed. That is that they may boldly to do all things by God's Word; may compel all worldly power, wisdom, and exaltation to yield to and obey his majesty." Calvin, *Institutes of the Christian Religion,* IV, VII, 9, p. 1156. But in his view, and contrary to the apostles, pastors cannot always claim to be guided by the Holy Spirit. This major weakness means that their authority is necessarily vulnerable, uncertain, and provisional.

21. See Groupe des Dombes, *Le ministère de communion dans l'Eglise universelle* (Paris: Centurion, 1986), no. 12, note 19.

22. John Paul II, *"Ut Unum Sint:* Encyclical on Commitment to Ecumenism," in *Origins* 25 (June 8, 1995): no. 95, p. 69.

terms of the present age. To use their cherished classical distinction between the visible and invisible church, one could say that the Protestant churches relegated the concept of apostolic succession[23] to the background of the shop window of visible unity. The churches of the Reformation could apply the principle of ambivalence and of "simultaneity" (Luther's *simul-simul*)[24] more rigorously to their understanding of the church in its visible and invisible, institutional and spiritual reality.[25]

470. "On the Protestant side . . . one often sees in practice that *unity* is regarded as an aggregate of diversities which at best tolerate each other, each jealous of its autonomy and its customs."[26] A consequence of the fragmentation of those churches born of the Reformation is a confessional isolation which is prejudicial to the unity of the church as it is conceived in Scripture. That is why these churches are called to abandon the idea that the already existing unity of the invisible church could justify a simple juxtaposition of the churches, at the expense of seeking a genuinely visible communion within which the gospel is proclaimed with renewed authority. Peaceful coexistence is not yet unity.

---

23. There is no need to reconsider the question of apostolic succession here with its two complementary constituents: the apostolic succession of the whole church and apostolic succession in the ministry instituted by the Lord. See our previous reflections in Groupe des Dombes, "Towards a Reconciliation of Ministries," in *Modern Ecumenical Agreements on Ministry*, ed. H. R. McAdoo (London: SPCK, 1973), nos. 10 and 11; and "The Episcopal Ministry: Reflections and Proposals Concerning the Ministry of Vigilance and Unity in the Particular Church," *One in Christ* 14 (1978): 267-288. See also Faith and Order, *Baptism, Eucharist and Ministry* (Geneva: WCC, 1982), nos. M34-M38.

24. See no. 368 above.

25. "In fact, such a distinction is not part of genuine Reformed teaching. We can affirm together the indissoluble link between the invisible and the visible. There exists but one Church of God. . . . Christ, through his Spirit, has empowered this Church for a mission and a ministry in the world. . . . From its earliest time, it has been provided through God's grace with ministerial means necessary and sufficient for the fulfillment of its mission." "Towards a Common Understanding of the Church," in *Growth in Agreement II*, ed. Jeffrey Gros, Harding Meyer, and William G. Rusch (Grand Rapids: Eerdmans/Geneva: WCC, 2000), no. 126, pp. 808-809. This reflection from the Reformed-Roman Catholic International Dialogue invites Protestants to a deeper understanding of a distinction that is misperceived and serves as an apparently irrefutable ready alibi. We wish to repeat here the invitation to debate.

26. Groupe des Dombes, *For the Conversion of the Churches*, no. 190.

3. The Difficult Question of Infallibility

471. The question of the church's infallibility and, in particular, of papal infallibility remains a subject of serious difference between us. Nonetheless, we would lose all credibility with our readers were we to keep silent on the matter.[27] From now on we must work together to resolve this problem.

472. Let us recall what was explained in the previous chapter[28] and must be kept in mind if the reader is to arrive at a correct understanding of the dogma of *infallibility*. Infallibility belongs first and foremost to the whole church, in the sense that it serves as guarantor of the apostolic faith. It is by virtue of the church's infallibility — and more generally of its indefectibility[29] — that it can and must take a position against affirmations that would harm the content of the gospel. The interpretation of the dogma of papal infallibility must take account of historical and theological facts outlined above.[30] There is no question of an "absolute" infallibility, nor of a "personal" infallibility, and certainly not of a "separate" infallibility.[31]

473. Bear in mind also the affirmation that the notion of the church's infallibility is receivable in a Protestant context. It concerns the church's witness to the gospel. For Luther, the faithful preaching of the gospel ("hear what the Lord is saying," *Haec dicit Dominus!*) is infalli-

27. To be sure, we readily acknowledge that the formal exercise of papal infallibility is not a topical question in the Catholic Church, which has only seen one case of such an intervention since Vatican I. Yet it remains symbolically sensitive and painful. For this reason, we do not wish to avoid it.

28. See above, nos. 387-388.

29. The exercise of infallibility implies the irreformable character of the meaning affirmed on the doctrinal theme in question. Indefectibility does not necessarily imply such irreformability. It merely indicates that the church was not wrong in proposing a reformable doctrine, that is to say, with regard to its saving mission.

30. See above, nos. 196-199.

31. See above, nos. 203-206. "For the Holy Spirit was promised to the successors of Peter not so that they might, by his revelation, make known some new doctrine, but that, by his assistance, they might religiously guard and faithfully expound the revelation deposit of faith transmitted by the apostles." First Vatican Council, "First Dogmatic Constitution on the Church of Christ [*Pastor Aeternus*]," in *Decrees of the Ecumenical Councils,* vol. 2, ed. Norman P. Tanner (London: Sheed and Ward/Georgetown: Georgetown University Press, 1990), no. 4, p. 816.

ble. Yet this remains a partial consensus because it is counterbalanced by the application of the affirmation "at the same time justified and sinner" to the church, and the disagreement concerning an infallibility entrusted to human persons. Infallibility is about God's fidelity to the covenant with humanity in spite of error and of failure on the part of human beings in keeping God's Word. While the Reformers' distinction between the "visibility" and the "invisibility" of the church is intended to underscore the paradoxical duality of its reality, Protestant ecclesiology can affirm that the church is infallible in the spiritual body of Christ, in the certitude that it enjoys the presence of the Spirit in the contemporary expression of its apostolic mission. Paradoxically, this ecclesiology is able to say, at the same time, that the church is nonetheless fallible in its historical reality, in the certitude that it always has need of repentance from its weakness and from the "fallibility" of the human witness rendered to the gospel of Jesus Christ.

474. It is our hope that the infallibility recognized as belonging to the papal magisterium only be practiced in very exceptional situations. For example, in a case where the bishop of Rome would have no possibility of consulting the episcopate, he would be authorized in conscience to intervene concerning a serious disagreement in matters of faith, by reason of the office he has received and his responsibility in the service of ecclesial unity. In these very situations, the bishop of Rome could not act without presupposing the agreement of the bishops who are in communion with him. Such an interpretation of the Catholic dogma is respectful of its genuine meaning and appears necessary in the perspective of ecclesial unity.

475. Similarly, we ask that the existence of this dogma not result in a surreptitious overvaluation of the authority of pontifical documents and those of the Roman curia. We ask that the faithful be encouraged to discern the different degrees of authority implied by these documents, notably because of the impact of the media in the presentation of religious news items.

476. It is our hope that the Catholic Church might, in the near future, undertake a reformulation of the dogma of papal infallibility so that it might be more clearly situated within an ecclesiology of communion. This reformulation could take place in the context of a future council where delegates from other churches would play an important role.

477. While it awaits this clarification, the Catholic Church would maintain the practice of only engaging papal infallibility in exceptional cases, after a consultation of the whole church which could be enlarged to include the other churches. For their part, the churches of the Reformation could accept this dogma as binding for their Catholic brothers and sisters, even if, according to the Reformation perspective, it does not belong to the order of the truths of faith.

478. We ask that the churches of the Reformation not consider every exercise of the papal magisterium as infallible. This confusion of various forms of teaching is both erroneous and dangerous. Almost all papal interventions — when he is not repeating the traditional affirmations of creedal faith — belong only to the order of the authentic magisterium.[32]

We also request, as we have done so previously,[33] that the churches of the Reformation face resolutely the question of the ministry of unity for the whole church.

Section V: The Interrelationship of Authority

479. This final theme brings together all the previous ones, for it concerns their interrelationship. Relationships of superiority and subordination, however necessary, are radically transformed by the newness that is at the very heart of the gospel. They are to be lived out "in the Lord" and ordered to the communion of Christians, which has its source in the relationship of the Father with the Son in the unity of the Spirit. "Truly our fellowship is with the Father and with his son Jesus Christ" (1 John 1:3).[34]

480. Authority is thus not to be understood as the right of certain Christians over others (2 Cor. 1:24), but rather as a service entrusted by the Lord so that the members of the body share the same faith and so that, through the quality of their mutual relations, they witness together to the one who became a Servant. The main idea is the correct balance between the "top-down" and "bottom-up" movements in the

---

32. The term is defined above, nos. 215-216.
33. See *Le Ministère de communion dans l'Église universelle,* no. 157.
34. See above, no. 293.

regulation of the faith. The Catholic Church has favored a top-down approach. The churches of the Reformation favor a bottom-up approach. Conversion is required on both sides, in opposing directions. Having said that, we can now address the churches together, indicating several points for conversion.

481. *(The Regulation of the Faith)* The exercise of doctrinal authority requires *procedures of regulation that serve ecclesial communion.* This institutional regulation should be accepted by all and enable the participation of all. It requires the specific contribution of the local and regional churches, their theologians, and their pastors. It must "flow" in a reciprocal movement of give and take among the authorities and the people of God.

482. The regulation of faith must be exercised with an acute sense of unity in faith and the communion of all Christians. For Catholics, the ministry of the bishop of Rome must be understood as a ministry of unity and of communion, not only for the good of the Catholic Church but in the perspective of communion among all the baptized.[35] His authority finds its meaning in the framework of a church that is a communion of churches. For Protestants, the sense of faith must include more broadly the realization of a genuine communion of churches held together by visible bonds and an authority at the level of the universal church.

483. *(Plurality of Cultures)* The plurality of living cultures in the churches throughout the world raises new questions concerning the regulation of the faith. It implies on one hand, a confrontation between churches within a single cultural area, and, on the other hand, an exchange concerning the formulation of the faith from one cultural space to the next. The local and regional churches have an essential role to play in such a process. At the same time, such a process has a greater requirement for a ministry of presiding and of unity to watch over its coherence.

484. *(The Manner of Teaching)* The authors of the Gospels draw our attention to the ways in which Jesus chose to teach his disciples and the crowds: through parables and discourses. The *parable* is a language of

---

35. As Pope John Paul II recalled: "Whatever relates to the unity of all Christian communities clearly forms part of the concerns of the primacy." *"Ut Unum Sint,"* no. 95, p. 69.

questioning, openness, and freedom. Because of this, there are those who hear and those who do not hear, a relationship or a refusal of relationship between Jesus and those who listen. The word of Jesus, which is true, has authority only when it is received, welcomed, and recognized as a word that accomplishes that to which we are invited.

Jesus also teaches through the use of a *discourse* that ought not to be separated from the fabric of the story. The link between the two reveals that this "doctrine" is about liberation, healing, and forgiveness. In the Gospel of Matthew, the first discourse begins with the Beatitudes, words that declare and promise the happiness and joy of the Kingdom. These ways of speaking are part of the truth that is being communicated and enable us to recognize the authority of the words.

485. We ask that all of our churches speak more "to the heart" of their faithful and to the men and women of our time, that they speak an encouraging word capable of inspiring "pilgrims" of faith on their journey. It is hoped that the form of witness, the proclamation of the Good News, and the call to true joy will awaken the desire to believe and balance out the inevitable reminders of the norms. In catechesis, let due consideration be given to the accessibility of the faith and development in faith in a pedagogy that leads to an integral understanding of the faith.

486. *(Differentiated Consensus)* We return to the method of differentiated consensus often referred to in these pages. Rather than seek the same ordering and the same ensemble of doctrinal elements, are we not being invited to *discern* together *how* and *how much each of our complex and original doctrinal corpuses testifies and refers to the "foundation"*? Does this not open the door to the possibility of entering into communion with other churches which have different types of doctrinal coherence? The fact that John Paul II called the Assyrian Church of the East, a church which shares neither the same canon of Scriptures nor seven sacraments, a "sister church"[36] reveals the benefit of such an approach.[37] We can grow together toward a model of unity that assumes the logic of the differentiated consensus which we are able to achieve today.

---

36. "Common Christological Declaration between the Catholic Church and the Assyrian Church of the East [1994]," in *Growth in Agreement II*, pp. 711-712.

37. Hervé Legrand, "Le consensus différencié et la doctrine de la justification. Augsbourg 1999," *Nouvelle Revue Théologique* 124 (2002): 45, note 31.

Conclusion: In Service of a Unity
That Is Both a Gift and a Task

487. The New Testament testifies to the unity of Christians following the death of Jesus and rooted in the unity of Jesus with God (John 17:11, 21-22) and to the fact that that the body of Christ is one (Rom. 12:5; 1 Cor. 12:13, 27; Gal. 3:28), for Christ is not divided (1 Cor. 1:13), just as there is but one Spirit (1 Cor. 12:4; Eph. 4:4). Thus, the unity of the church is given prior to any human effort to heal existing fractures and promote full communion among the churches.[38] *Discourse on unity, then, takes on a dialectical character. As soon as one affirms the presence of unity, one must add that it not yet fully realized, and while we await its coming, one must specify that its very presence is the basis of all waiting.*

In this perspective, conversion toward a broader interpretation of the unity of the church consists in listening to and in appropriating other voices in the universal church that testify to the inexhaustible riches of the gospel. Because the unity of the church points to the unity of the saving work of Jesus Christ who died and is risen, it remains at once hidden and in the form of a promise: hidden, for it stands in the shadow of the cross; promised, because it will only be fully revealed when the Easter light has definitively dissipated the darkness of the sin of humanity. As in the beginning, unity will then be a gift. In the meantime, the task of the church is to build unity and to live it as a sign of the future coming of the Kingdom. Anything less would be a denial of its privileged vocation in the service of the world and of humanity.

---

38. "The holy mystery of oneness, this unbreakable bond of close-knit harmony, is portrayed in the gospel by our Lord Jesus Christ's coat, which is not divided or cut at all, but when they drew lots for the vesture of Christ to see which of them should win out on Christ, it was the whole coat that was won, the garment was acquired unspoiled and undivided." Saint Cyprian, "The Unity of the Catholic Church," in *Ancient Christian Writers*, vol. 25, ed. J. Quaesten and J. Plumpe (Westminster, Md.: Newman Press/London: Longman, Green and Co., 1957), p. 49.

Conclusion

488. We must now conclude this study, which has attempted in a loyal manner to take stock of the ways in which our traditions have evolved in expressing doctrinal authority. Together we have reexamined the Scriptures, that which fundamentally unites us in the affirmation of doctrine, and the ways we differ in the practice and exercise of authority. It is not possible to offer a definitive conclusion, given the complexity of the subject and the fact that it goes to the very heart of the lives of our churches throughout their ongoing development.

Nonetheless, we are *convinced of two things:*

489. In a society like ours, where reference points are becoming more and more blurred, where individualism readily carries the day over any reference to the community in the name of conscience, and where personal and collective hope is not exactly flourishing, it is more urgent than ever for the churches to proclaim their faith and to demonstrate their deepest convictions. Perhaps, in our minority context, we are living in an age that is comparable to that of the early church with its courageous witnesses and martyrs, but which does not rule out an authoritative word in the name of the faith that enlivens us. Let us not, however, forget that "being authoritative" in this age, as in the time of Christ, will always have the nature of a convincing and convinced proposition, and not of a hegemonic imposition.

490. If it is true, as this study has demonstrated, that one must not confuse doctrinal authority with the institutional forms of its exercise, both Catholic and Protestant churches still have a long road of challenging and fraternal dialogue ahead. One of the greatest ecumenical

questions of today and of tomorrow, the question before all of our churches in this time of rediscovered fellowship, will be that of recognizing the ecclesiality of other churches. So long as the churches each determine their own criteria of genuine ecclesiality or of the correct exercise of the magisterium, so long as each church diminishes its ecclesiological justification and underscores what is lacking or excessive in others, we will remain unable to break present ecumenical deadlocks, or to progress toward the unity promised and already given in Christ.

491. We have observed that we are united on a number of fundamental points of faith concerning authoritative texts and on the role of doctrinal authority. With regard to the exercise of that authority, our churches put the same elements into play but according to different reasoning, organizations, and juridical ordering. For that reason, they must find a way to determine together the criteria of ecclesiality. Under what conditions could our churches mutually recognize each other as "sister churches"? This is the great task ahead for ecumenical dialogue. All of this should give us the courage to undertake without delay a critical examination of our respective traditions, of their exaggerations and weaknesses, of their particular emphases, and of the caricatures they still carry of other churches.

492. For a long time now the Groupe des Dombes has been calling for the "conversion of the churches." It comes through in each of its studies as a pressing call addressed to every Christian and to the churches in their common and institutional life. It is a matter of everyone making a genuine effort to "turn around," going far beyond the world of good feelings, abandoning the secure shores of our certitudes to find the deep waters of a new spiritual fecundity, without renouncing the best of one's particular tradition.

493. Many of the proposals in this text point toward a still distant horizon. Discernment and vigilance are required so these proposals for conversion do not become inaccessible and ineffective dreams. Intermediate steps and objectives must be considered. But from this day forward the journey has begun; everyone can make the road easier and hasten the arrival at our goal. The openness and transformation of the churches begins with that of every Christian, every parish, and every group, ecumenical or not. An understanding of a doctrinal authority more in conformity with the gospel, and the mutual recognition of our

respective ecclesialities, will also depend upon the quality of our encounters and of our collaboration.

494. An experience of conversion "thanks to the other" requires, at the very least and wherever we live in proximity with each other, that we no longer confuse ecumenism with a simple peaceful coexistence. It always presupposes the sharing of faith and common prayer, sharing in the joys and sufferings of each church, a necessary conversion of our language, and without limiting all this to the one week a year where we recall this more intensely, the Week of Prayer for Christian Unity.

We must therefore multiply the opportunities that allow us to experience and appreciate the ecclesiality of the other[1] and take decisions in common whenever possible.[2]

495. As we have stated in our study of doctrinal authority and after the publication of so many texts by commissions for official theological dialogue, this change of perspective, this "turning back," and this conversion are essential to the cause of unity. The late Bruno Chenu concluded his final book as follows:

> Every Christian is called to be a "universal little brother" or a "universal little sister" wherever they live. It would be a wonderful contribution if globalization were to open each human being to the possibility of an identity based, not on opposition and exclusion, but on relationship with others, in the awareness of a legitimate otherness and of an indelible resemblance, so that ultimately, in a Pauline or Irenaean dynamic, "God may be all in all" (1 Cor 15:28).[3]

We make this our prayer and struggle as well, as we work together and individually in the life of our churches.

---

1. See Conference of European Churches (KEK) and the Council of European Episcopal Conferences (CCEE), "Charta Oecumenica," nos. 2-7. http://www.cec-kek.org/content/charta.html.

2. Jean M. Tillard, "Quelle communion?" *Documents Épiscopat* 8 (juin 1995).

3. Bruno Chenu, *L'Église sera-t-elle catholique?* (Paris: Bayard, 2004), p. 159.

The following participated in the elaboration of this text in the course of meetings from 1999 to 2004 at the Abbey of Pradines:

Père Jean-Noël Aletti
Pasteur François Altermath
Père René Beaupère
Père Yves-Marie Blanchard
Pasteur Daniel Bourguet
Père Dominique Cerbelaud
Pasteur Marc Chambron
Père Jean-François Chiron
Pasteur Gill Daudé
Père Michel Deneken
Père Claude Ducarroz
Sœur Françoise Durand
Père Michel Fédou
Pasteur Flemming Fleinert-Jensen
Père Christian Forster
Pasteur Michel Freychet
Pasteur Daniel Fricker
Père Paul Gay
Pasteur Gottfried Hammann

Père Joseph Hoffmann
Sœur Nathanaël Kirchner
Pasteur Guy Lasserre
Père Pierre Lathuilière
Pasteur Michel Leplay
Père Michel Mallèvre
Pasteur Alain Massini
Sœur Christianne Meroz
Pasteur Willy-René Nussbaum
Pasteur Elisabeth Parmentier
Pasteur Jacques-Noël Pérès
Sœur Anne-Marie Petitjean
Père Pierre Remise
Père Louis-Michel Renier
Pasteur Antoine Reymond
Père Bernard Sesboüé
Pasteur Jean Tartier
Pasteur Geoffroy de Turckheim
Pasteur Denis Vatinel
Pasteur Gaston Westphal